Designated Driver

Michelle Smith

Tiny Street Publishing
www.tinystreetpublishing.com

Published in 2013 by Tiny Street Publishing
www.tinystreetpublishing.com
Printed in the USA, Gorham Printing

ISBN: 978-0-9896482-0-2

Cover Artwork: Michelle Smith
Cover Design: Julie Handel, askjulie.com
Cover Photography: Mariette Hart
Author Photograph: Mariette Hart

To Rick—my husband, my love, my best friend.

"In all this you greatly rejoice, though now for a little while you may have had to suffer grief in all kinds of trials. These have come so that the proven genuineness of your faith—of greater worth than gold, which perishes even though refined by fire—may result in praise, glory and honor when Jesus Christ is revealed."

1 Peter 1:5–7

Contents

Crash

"I have told you these things, so that in me you may have peace. In this world you will have trouble. But take heart! I have overcome the world."
John 16:33

Chapter 1 - Beginnings

By eighteen, my grandmother was married to the tall, skinny boy who had been her neighbor since she was just three years old. Everyone in their small town said they would get married someday. As long as anyone could remember, they had been inseparable. There had never been a day that Horace could not remember being in love with Lila June. It had never occurred to Lila that she had any other option; that is, until she met Willard—my grandfather.

My grandpa was born a twin. On November 16, 1918, Willard Raymond and Lillard Namon came into the world. Lillard would only live a short time before dying on December 4. My grandfather would die on that same day sixty-five years later. Being part Cherokee, but mostly Irish, my grandfather would joke that he never had a chance of getting too far from a whiskey bottle. And, that is why my grandfather spent most of his time in bars, and when he wasn't there, he was in jail. When he was out of jail and sober, he was like a well-chiseled statue— tall and strong from farm work and fighting. He had black hair and sky-blue eyes. His skin was golden when he worked in the fields and my grandmother said he dressed like Cary Grant.

As for going to jail, my grandpa liked to fight. His propensity for fighting began when he was just sixteen years old. When he was ten years old, he lived in a small town in Arkansas. His family was so poor that they couldn't afford shoes. His own father had never found steady work or a vocation. Sometimes my grandfather and his siblings would tie cardboard to their feet, but most of the time they were barefoot.

According to my grandpa, there were two other boys from his school who were rich, or at least wealthy enough to have bicycles and shoes. They would chase my grandfather home on their bikes and try to run over his bare toes. Being sickly from asthma, my grandfather would run breathlessly home from being chased, his chest heaving as he ran up the broken wooden steps into his dilapidated home for escape: a rabbit on the run. Eventually, my grandpa's family moved from that place to Idaho, in hopes of curing my grandfather's asthma. It worked, and six year later my grandpa went back to Arkansas one summer to help his family on their farm. He was strong, tall, and powerful now. He hunted those two boys down and when he found them, he beat them up, and then, made them eat a pile of horse manure that was heaped in the street. He said after that he was changed forever. He never missed an opportunity to start, end, or get into the middle of a fight: it strengthened him in all the wrong ways.

My grandmother may have seen Cary Grant, but surely the townspeople of Jerome, Idaho, saw only a troublemaker. This newcomer never stopped fighting or drinking. His escapades became newsworthy. My mother even had a newspaper clipping titled, "Man Eludes Police on Horseback." That my grandfather tamed a wild horse and rode it to town on Friday and Saturday nights only made sense because Reno, the horse, was smart enough to either make it back to the farm, or run from a police car after a barroom brawl. If my grandfather got arrested, Reno would eventually wander home alone without any rider at all. Some people train horses to perform in circuses – my grandfather trained Reno to be an outlaw.

It wasn't long before my grandparents met. My grandmother, Lila, worked at a dime store. She had been a majorette in school and marched in the high school marching band. She and Horace had gotten married before high school ended and lived simply in their simple town. When World War II broke out, Horace was quick to enlist. Soon, Horace shipped out and Lila was left alone.

It wasn't long before Willard noticed Lila. She would have been hard to ignore. She was beautiful. She had creamy skin and lush auburn hair that curled and tucked at the nape of her long elegant neck. Her stride was confidant and poised—well beyond her eighteen years and exceedingly out of the norm in a small town. She was, by all standards, out of Willard's league. It didn't matter though because he was not easily daunted. He began visiting her at the dime store, and before long they were stealing away, hiding their feelings from the townspeople, and indulging in a full-blown love affair.

After just two months of dating, Lila became pregnant. Fortunately for Willard, he had already gotten his deployment papers. As the heat turned up, he flew away, denying he'd even known Lila. Whatever grace she'd been granted for her imperial stature in that town was now in a heap of ashes. Lila, my grandmother, was now considered the town whore, defiled by the only person who could possibly be worse than her, the town drunk.

It would play out that the ladies of the town, those women who had once felt so inferior to her, would now openly mock her. Their husbands would steal lingering glances and make vulgar advances, for if their wives found out, they could just as easily blame it on the girl with the scarlet letter. Who would believe her anyway?

And, in light of my grandfather's denial, Horace returned home from war and without concern for being a laughingstock, claimed paternity for my mother—a child that, with the whole town's knowledge, had been conceived behind his back with another man.

12

Still, Lila longed for Willard, and in truth, Willard longed for her too. Though he had been terrified at having conceived a child with another man's wife, he could not forsake his love for Lila, though he would try to forget her, leave her to her husband, and relinquish the baby to a stable life. Lila would outwardly shrug off her so-called mistake and wait patiently for true love to come home and find her.

When my grandfather came home from his deployment in the Aleutian Islands, to Jerome, a town of only 3,000 people, he could only avoid Lila and Horace for so long. With just a handful of diners, it wasn't long until they ended up in the same one. He tried to ignore the threesome settled into a corner booth—Lila, her illegitimate child, Lena, and Lila's weak, cuckolded husband, Horace. As the entire diner froze and awaited a response, Willard's friend whispered to him to ignore them and sit at the counter.

"Ignore 'em," he prodded, elbowing Willard in the side. My grandfather, Willard, tried, but the baby became suddenly agitated and seemed to cry out to him, her tiny hands grasping at the air, her back arching over Lila's tight embrace. The baby would not be quiet, as though she sensed some looming excitement, like a horse spooked by a snake hidden in the brush.

Even then, in his most raucous state, Willard had a soft heart for children. He readjusted uncomfortably on the stiff red leather stool and planted his two elbows on the green Formica countertop. As everybody watched, he slowly lit a cigarette and let the smoke exhale into a stream upward toward the stark tin ceiling. He needed to be sure. He had to know, was this his baby? With all eyes on him, he casually glanced over his shoulder at the crying baby, expecting and hoping to see nothing, no recognition at all, but in an instant, in that fleeting glance, he knew he saw himself. In a rush of realization, he saw the precocious shimmer of her blue-gray eyes, the slender shape of her face, the tuft of russet curls along her cheeks: It appeared to him that his little sister, Dotty, squirmed for him in Lila's arms. Dotty. Dotty, who had died years before because of a kitten he had innocently brought her as a plaything. A plaything that would give Dotty diphtheria until a fever overtook her one night and she died in his mother's arms. Yes, that baby Lila struggled with looked exactly like Dotty. His mind struggled with images of Dotty and he inhaled again deeply on his cigarette, trying to stabilize his thoughts.

When Dotty died, his mother never recovered. His alcoholic father beat him repeatedly for it, though he was sure it was just an excuse for hearty beatings rather than righteous retaliation. Because Willard knew that his father had already begun touching Dotty, caressing her inappropriately. He had seen the low gaslight stream from her room late at night, heard his father come and go like a thief. Willard knew. He knew because his father had done that to all of his sisters. At five, Dotty had just begun her initiation process. Had diphtheria not taken her, she would have had years of it. When that was over, there would have been beatings—beatings for this and beatings for that. The torture would have never ended, but Dotty escaped. To Willard, she would always be an angel hovering just beyond reach.

And now, he felt nearly certain Dotty had come back to him in the form of his own daughter. His mind whirled at the idea of it. His eyes rested on the baby and then on Lila. He longed for Lila all over again. His heart pounded nearly out of his chest. He missed her. He needed her. He could not live without her. As though his mind no longer worked, his heart told him to stand and go get her. Go get them both.

Moved by something greater than himself, he stood and walked to Lila and her child—his child. He did not even see Horace. Horace had always been invisible. Willard reached for Lila's hand. Her heart almost shot through her chest. Her prince had come, at last. Inexplicably drawn to him, as she'd always been, her small, delicate hand met his, and with my mother in her other arm, she stood. It seemed the entire

14

diner was suspended in the moment, like a stone slowly sinking to the bottom of a jar of molasses. They walked out. The only sound was the clicking of their shoes on the black and white tiles. Surely, Horace had known all along that it was just a matter of time. He hung his head and began to cry. He did not bother getting up. He did not bother watching his wife walk away with the man she loved. He was too consumed by the gulping contractions of his broken heart trying to rush after her.

The day that my grandfather took my grandmother by the hand began a long, tumultuous life for my grandparents, my mother, and her three siblings, who were still to come—Nanny, Bess and Rita. My grandfather would be in and out of jail countless times. And his father would take advantage of the turmoil to molest my mother and her sisters as many times as he could.

One day, as my grandfather lay sprawled across his bed, his eye blackened and swollen shut, still too drunk to move, my grandmother left for California with his best friend, Clyde. She would pry my mother off of him, as my mom begged him to wake. "Daddy, Daddy, wake up! Wake up!" My aunts, my mother's two younger sisters, Nanny and Bess, sat as upright as schoolgirls in the backseat of the getaway car, tears streaming down their cheeks. Willard could barely hear and he could not move. The last sound he heard was the slamming of a door. He would awake hours later to find things strewn about, drawers and closets emptied. He was alone.

In the months to come, my grandmother would wind up pregnant by Clyde, and then, on one cheery, sunny California spring day, my grandfather showed up unexpectedly at their door. According to my mother, then thirteen years old, she would fall apart, cling to him, and cry, "Never leave! Never, ever leave, Daddy!"

It wasn't long before my grandmother took him back. This was their final separation and reconciliation, and Clyde would slink away, more quietly and even less proudly than Horace, even though my

15

grandmother was carrying and would eventually have Clyde's child.

Chapter 2 - My Other Side

My father was born in California, but my paternal grandparents, Naoma and Bill, came from Oklahoma. Flung out of that barren state by a dust storm, they were blown asunder like a jagged, pokey tumbleweed. They landed in the flat and yellow hard-baked San Joaquin Valley, like ants wandering over a large flat pan of golden cornbread. As farmers, they found comfort in the elements there: the smell of manure on the swirling wind, the rows and rows of something reaching through the dirt toward the sky, the big expanse of blue canopy overhead, and the hope that something could come from the nothing underfoot. Yes, they were Okies, brought to California by the Dust Bowl.

My grandmother was the most overlooked person in her family. Falling in the middle, as my father would, she was more a workhorse than a cherished, dainty girl. She told me that she, and no animal, pulled the plow through their fields. With a shy, quiet demeanor, she was easily smitten by my charming and outgoing grandfather. My grandmother had a halo of flaxen hair, a peaches-and-cream complexion, and light blue eyes, as tender as an Oklahoma sunrise. My grandfather had a darker complexion and dark, wavy hair that he would oftentimes run his fingers through. His eyes were bright and the blue in them danced with his jovial nature and enthusiastic laughter. Coming from a strict Southern Baptist upbringing, with a preacher as a father, my grandmother was not encouraged to engage with my grandfather at all. She told me that when she could, she sneaked away from her chores and met my grandfather at a fencepost under a large, expansive redbud tree, just out of sight of her overbearing father. There, my grandpa told her how beautiful she was and how he would marry her someday. Grandma would call him "dearest darling," and tell him she wanted to be married to him more than anything in the world.

My grandfather was in stark contrast to everything my grandmother's father wanted for her. He was fun and gregarious, and sadly, without any impressive family connection to church, God, or theology. His mother had died giving birth to his younger brother, Milton, when my grandfather was just five years old. Though my grandpa couldn't have known his mother well, I recall him crying for his mama well into his adulthood as he pulled me onto his lap, brushed the tears from his sad eyes, and said, "Sometimes, Shelly, you just want your mama." I never understood that until I was older.

My grandfather also said that he always asked my grandma first to the town dances, but when she couldn't go, he would be "forced" to ask another girl. His heart, he said, was always waiting for Naoma, and oftentimes, after he told me that story, he would grab my grandmother and plant a big kiss on her lips. She would blush, pull away, and say, "Oh, Bill," and they would laugh. I'll be honest, just writing that makes me cry at how cruel time can be because I miss them every day. At the time, I acted as though it was disgusting, but secretly, I loved the way they loved each other and was thankful to be in their presence.

When they began their life together, they were painfully poor. My Aunt Clara, my dad's oldest sibling and only sister, was born in a tent. My Uncle Bruce, two years younger than my aunt, was born breach. The doctor who delivered him was drunk, and instead of turning him prior to pulling him from my grandmother's womb, he simply pulled on my uncle's infant legs until he was irreparably crippled. Though he went through countless surgeries, he never walked without the use of crutches. My father, born five years later, said that when he was a child, Bruce would crawl, pulling himself over the dry stubbly ground of the San Joaquin Valley.

For most of Bruce's youth, he lived at St. Jude's hospital in San Francisco. With great fear and trepidation, my grandparents signed over their parental rights to the hospital. With only a drying shed and a packed dirt floor as a home, they knew the sterile nature of a hospital was a far better home than what they could provide for Bruce.

Life had proven to be a daily struggle for my grandparents, and at some point my father was left to fend for himself. I'm sure it wasn't the way my grandparents wanted it, but some things are inescapable. In the midst of daily drudgeries, my grandmother could not lavish my father with the love he desperately needed. Instead, she remained aloof toward him, maybe out of self-preservation. What if one more thing went wrong with one of her children? How could she persevere? No, my grandmother, though one day she would impart me with care, affection, and steadfast love, could barely tell my father she loved him, without an amendment of how her feelings were stronger for his younger brother. Yes, even though one day she would be my favorite, and I hers, she was strangely void toward my father.

When I was four years old, I saw my twenty-five-year-old dad cry and beg my grandmother for her love. "Please," he cried, tears streaming down his face, "Why can't you just tell me you love me? Why?" He stood there, as she peered at him from her porch, unable to be more— unable to lavish him with love. My grandfather came from the house, took her by the hand, and they quietly closed and locked the door, while my dad openly wept for an answer. My poor dad, rejected again and again. It never seemed to change. When my grandma was well-aged one day, and my grandfather was dead, my father went to her house every day to visit her, and always, she was reserved toward him—kind and gentle, but carefully stoic and distant.

Outwardly, my father said nothing, but inwardly, he seethed contempt like a pot forgotten on the stove that becomes blackened with heaps of bubbled-up soot. In his youth, he worked alongside my grandparents, picking prunes, apricots, walnuts, and cotton—cotton was the worst, always the worst. With a small, soft, white tuft on the end of a rough, brown, crumpled bud, the thorny branches snagged and ripped his fingers. At the end of a long day, in the heat of the baking sun, my father's young, plump fingers became bloody and torn.

Living among wealthy farmers and landowners and their overly indulged children, it didn't take long for my father's resentment to build. He was angry that they were so poor. He was angry that poverty did not propel his parents to work harder, faster, and with greater zeal for riches and wealth. If they could not give him love then they should give him something. When a kind-hearted farmer took pity on my grandparents and gave them an additional drying shed to attach to their older one, my father felt dread and shame at the idea that someone noticed their pitiable living conditions and showed them charity. He was disgraced to know that an entire community knew of their impoverished living conditions. He was angry that he had to work so hard for so little, while classmates enjoyed modern conveniences, like electricity, running water, inside toilets, and indoor flooring. It was 1958, and unlike the burgeoning world of progress, my father felt as though he had been dropped into a dismal abyss of belabored toil. He had become an essential income-earner to his family, like an ox that pulls the heaviest weight, but seldom gets the credit. His work ethic was solidly cast and he would never be an idle man.

Eventually, my grandfather found work as a carpenter in the developing Santa Clara Valley, which later became Silicon Valley. In 1961 my father's family moved to a mountainous area above the lush valley floor, and finally they had indoor plumbing, flooring that wasn't dirt, and a house made from real building materials, not a single-layered plywood shed meant for drying vegetables and storing farming equipment. It was that summer, the summer of 1961, that my parents met.

My mother was a pretty, seventeen-year-old brunette with hair that looked like Jackie Kennedy's and a svelte figure that was tall, lean, and tanned. Her eyes sparkled with a cheerful nature. She loved nothing more than engaging others in her frivolous fun times. Just being with her made you feel more exciting and carefree. Having come from a questionable lineage, she was strangely innocent, strangely untouched, and strangely pure. It was as though she had, for all appearances, shoved her family indiscretions under a bed far into a dark corner. No one would have known her father had spent so much time in jail. No one would have suspected that my beautiful mother and her three sisters had been molested by their own grandfather: no one would have suspected they were not a perfect family.

Unlike my outgoing, fun-loving mother, my father was brooding. He had virtually no sense of humor, which is often the case when a person has no ability for self-deprecating humor. To have laughed at his own shortcomings would have been too sensitive a topic, too self-effacing. Though his physical features were light, his heart was darkened by troubles that exceeded his ability to cope. He had red hair and green eyes that mimicked the California shoreline. In appearance, he was All-American, tall and handsome.

The day they met was glaringly bright. My mother was driving her parents' turquoise-green 1952 Buick Riviera. Her sisters, Nanny and Bess, were in the car too. Rita was just five years old and still too young to tag along. Bess was in the front seat. Her blonde hair was combed into large, looping curls. Her oversized white sunglasses hid her pretty blue eyes. She was singing softly to the radio. Nanny was in the backseat. Her dark hair was ratted high in a mound and the windows were down, as Nanny held her long, slender arm out the window lazily zigzagging it up and down in the wind.

"Slow down," Nanny purred. "What is this?" She turned in her seat.

"What's what?" Lena questioned. She slowed the car, turning just in time to see three young men get into a dark gray 1953 Chevy coupe in a parking lot.

"Turn around, turn around," Nanny ordered. "Right here." She pointed her finger over Lena's shoulder. "Turn right here."

Lena turned the car into the parking lot and the large vehicle lumbered slowly over the curb. The tall, redheaded boy was getting into his car, but not before he saw the three attractive girls driving slowly by. Nanny smiled and waved. She was not subtle in the art of flirtation.

Jack, my father, jumped into his car's black, cracked-leather seat and started the engine. It revved loudly, as he jerked the car into reverse and then spun forward.

Nanny turned halfway in her seat, and from the corner of her heavily kohl-encircled eye she saw the boys following them. "Stop. Stop the car, Lena." Abruptly the car jolted to a halt and just as abruptly, Jack rammed into the rear end.

"What? Why? Why did you say that? Why did you . . ." Lena was bewildered and flustered. She ran her hands quickly through her dark, wavy hair.

Jack came to her open window. "What are you doing? Why'd you just stop like that?" With both hands, he leaned onto the side of Lena's car and crossed his legs. He couldn't help but notice how pretty the driver was. To him, she looked just like Natalie Wood.

"I . . . I don't know. I was listening to Nanny . . . my sister." She nodded over her shoulder at Nanny who was leaning forward toward

Jack, smiling.

"Hellooo," Nanny cooed softly.

Meanwhile, Lena had begun to cry. Her nose was turning red and she wiped her eyes. "I need to call my dad," she whimpered.

"Why don't you pull over." Jack smiled. "Just park and we'll exchange information. You don't need to go calling your daddy."

Lena glared at him. She was quickly suspicious of anyone discouraging her from calling her parents.

"Yeah, Lena," Nanny piped in, "no need to call Daddy. We can handle this like adults." With one quick motion, Nanny had opened the door and was shutting it solidly with her backside. She drew close to Jack. Situating herself between Jack and the car, she pointed a long crimson fingernail to a place for Lena to park. "Lena, honey," she said as she let her arm droop across Jack's line of vision, "go park over there while we all figure this out."

Jack smiled at Nanny as she put her arm in his and walked him back to his car. "Now, you just park right next to her and let's work this thing out. What do you say?"

Jack jerked around his open car door and slid into the driver's seat. "Oh, I agree. Let's work it out." He shut the door and quickly started talking to his brother, Bruce. "Bruce, just stay in the car." Jack didn't want to chance the girls saying anything negative about Bruce and his crutches. "The driver . . . she's a real doll. The other one, this one," he nodded toward Nanny still smiling broadly through the closed glass, "she's a little too fast for me."

After Nanny ushered him into a parking stall, he turned to his friend in the backseat. "Tommy, why don't you talk to her? You can get out when we park here." He tugged the car into Park. "Man, I hope they don't go callin' their dad."

My mom did end up calling my grandfather. He and my grandmother made a trip to the parking lot where the accident happened. As it turned out, my grandparents were accustomed to responding to my mother's tearful calls, because at just eighteen, she had already been involved in numerous car accidents, or car-related mishaps. Once, she even ran over a boy she babysat! (No worries. He was fine.) Her car accidents were so commonplace that her nickname in her yearbook was "Crash." As she aged, road rage would have her slamming on her brakes, so that unsuspecting, tailgating Silicon Valley commuters would plunge into her rear bumper. Yes, my mother would be in countless, maybe as many as a hundred accidents, but this, this crash . . . it was different and it would change her life forever.

No matter how my Aunt Nanny flirted with my father, he knew instantly that he wanted my mother. Having a tough boy pretend to own you and be insanely jealous only made my mother more intrigued. After just three months of dating, they eloped to Las Vegas.

Surely, part of what attracted my father to my mom was the fact that when she was just eight years old, she had had kidney failure that appeared to make her barren. The doctor told my grandparents that my mother was going to die. Her family gathered around and made preparations. When she pulled through, the doctor told her she most likely would never be able to have children. For my father, that was just fine. Not having to expend emotions or money on children sounded tantalizingly scrumptious. When my older brother, Keith, was born nine months and twenty-four minutes after my parents married, you can imagine my father's dismay. It might explain why he started spanking my brother when Keith was just nine months old. Crying babies are especially annoying to someone who never expected any.

Then, just two years later came a girl—me. Now, being a girl in this situation is okay because my dad could not relate to me. He would pat me on the head every year or two, tell me I was pretty, and mosey on.

Unlike my brother, he did not attach himself to me like a barnacle on the underside of a ship. The upside was that I didn't carry his hopes or his failures: I was practically invisible. The downside is that I was practically invisible.

For my mother, having a boy was like having laid the golden egg. There were no boys in her family, so she pranced Keith around as if he had just slayed the village dragon. To her, he did nothing wrong: to my dad, he was innately wrong. In truth, my brother was a cute, blond-haired, blue-eyed, funny, affable, outgoing boy. He was far more charming than my father would ever be, and most notably, he was another male in direct competition with my father for my mother's affection.

When I was young, my brother was my hero. One time, when we were home alone—just thirteen and eleven—some boys broke into our house. In this day and age, I suppose it would be likened to a home invasion. Teenage boys pushed past my brother into our home, as he tried to fight them off. There were teenagers climbing over our backyard fence and our dog was sending them right back over with her snarling teeth. Terrified, but brave, my brother retrieved my father's loaded handgun and ran them off. I remember seeing him standing in the doorway, the gun in his hand. He was breathing heavily as he watched them flee from our house. He was terrified, but I was so proud of him because to me he was so brave. My dad got mad at him for that, but what were his options? No, I will never forget him standing there: The sunlight was illuminating his blond hair like a crown, and he was a hero.

In actuality, those boys had come for him. Just like my dad, they were jealous of Keith because he had so much to be jealous of. They were there to pulverize him, but because Keith was so likable in groups that mattered, it didn't take long for him to make a phone call here and mention something there, and pretty soon he had bona fide gang members terrorizing those impulsive idiotic teenage boys. His friend's brother gave word from jail to protect this funny white kid everyone liked, and just a couple of days later a mother of one of the boys who broke into our home was sitting on our living room sofa begging my mom and Keith to make it stop. Waah, waaah, waaah, they were afraid they were going to die. Uh, yeah, that's kind of how we felt when your lame kid came barging into our house, Cry Baby! But Keith was kind, and he called off the hounds.

In our own private hell, on numerous occasions, Keith would boldly place his body right between my parents' physical fights, taking the brunt of my father's abusive tirades. As best I could ascertain, my brother was fighting off the village dragon, but the delusional maiden kept letting the dragon back into the village, again and again.

As for me, I took a more practical approach to the dragon. To my mother's horror, I stated that if my father ever touched me, I'd call the police on him and have him arrested. The maiden did not like that scenario. In case that didn't scare him, I confided to my mother—in hopes she'd tell my dad—that if he ever hit me, I'd shoot him in his sleep. I suppose that was something he didn't want to chance because even though I was scared of him, and I would have most certainly been easy-pickings, he never hit me.

Eventually, things changed. My brother and I moved out and on with our lives. After college, I met Rick at a bar in San Francisco and we were engaged after just five months: When you know, you just know, even if you come to know in a bar. He is, by far, the best thing that has ever happened to me, except for my saving relationship with Jesus Christ. My relationship with Rick allowed me to grasp the idea of unconditional love. Prior to meeting him, that concept was much too abstract and I was far too jaded. I had been convinced that no man could love me, and I would never love a man so much, as to commit myself to one for a lifetime. With Rick's love and my burgeoning understanding of Christ, I was becoming someone with much greater confidence. In fact, I was beginning not to hate myself. It was changing my life—it was changing everything about me.

Still, in the rearview mirror was my mother, and for her nothing changed. She was left to deal with my father alone. I'd hear smatterings of violent episodes, but my mother had learned to cover up bruises and secrets with fantasy tales of her "love-hard-fight-hard" philosophy, romanticizing abusive dysfunction as the only mark of true love. At times my dad would call me and have me order yellow roses, as a peace offering after he had hit her. He would tell me what to say on the card. I'll never forget holding my son in my arms the last time my father called and I refused to do his bidding.

Austin was a toddler. I was busily making him something to eat and on the phone was my father telling me what he had done, in his coded way: "Your mom and I got in a bad fight last night. A real bad fight." That was code for, "I hit her," or "I choked her." He usually choked her. Sometimes, he would push her down the stairs. She would tell everyone she fell. If she had been choked, she would wear a turtleneck or a scarf.

I ran my fingers through Austin's red hair. He was a handsome little man. He looked so much like Rick. I kissed him on his sweet head.

"Yeah," my dad continued. "I have an account set up, so just go ahead and order those and have them sent to her work."

"Dad, I'm busy with Austin. Can't you do it yourself? You already have all the information."

"But . . ." he paused, "you've always done it."

That was true. I had always been dragged into their dysfunction. "Yeah, I know, but I'm married and have a child, and you shouldn't be fighting like that." The thought ran through my head: What would I do if Austin hit his wife someday? I quickly reckoned that I would drive however far to track him down, crawl through his bedroom window in the middle of the night, and beat him with a sock full of rocks. No matter how much I loved him, I would always expect him to be a man who loved and protected women, and would never, ever think of hurting a woman. I kissed him again and ran my hand over his plump cheeks.

"But . . ." My dad was stymied. "But, I'm busy."

"Dad, you're the one who needs to apologize for what you did and you should be the one to order the flowers, not me."

"Well, if that's how you feel," he said and abruptly hung up. He was mad. It wouldn't be the last time I made him angry. In fact, in just a few short years, he and I would argue almost incessantly. When I confronted my mom about drinking and driving with my kids in the car, my dad would call me and threaten to come over to my house and beat me up. I would tell him to hurry because the police don't like to be kept waiting.

It culminated in an ill-fated counseling appointment wherein my dad announced that they would drink and drive with our kids anytime they wanted, and I retorted in screams, "You'll never, ever do it with my kids in your car, so go on your stupid joy ride, idiot, and be sure to let me know where you're driving, so I can alert the police!" The police were always my threat because I had reasoned at an early age that people who act like criminals should be treated like criminals.

In that counselor's meeting, my dad also challenged me to hit him—a challenge that I mocked with the response: "Why don't you hit me, Jack? You're used to hitting girls." He then denied he had ever hit my mother, and my mom muttered under her breath that he was lying until he finally admitted to hitting her. But he added the cognitive sensitivity of using an open hand, rather than clenched fist, because in his words, "that would have killed her."

"How utterly humane," I taunted, "yeah, you're such a tough guy . . .

28

almost killing people with your mighty fist. What a laugh!" I'm sure the counselor thought we should all be euthanized.

The counseling appointment had essentially been arranged so we could find common ground, some way of coming together in a healthy way. I had already been going to counseling on my own with a counselor who specialized in alcoholic families. She had told me, almost warned me, that setting boundaries would be met with complete negativity. I would be made out to be one hundred percent horrible. She was right. As for me, there were basically three things I needed to confront my parents about in our counseling appointment: My mom's drinking, their lack of precaution with our children, and a painful incident that had happened in my twenties.

"I'm just afraid you'll end up like Aunt Nanny—dead from alcohol."

"That's not going to happen," my mom said soothingly as she patted my leg. "I just like to party sometimes."

"See, right there, right there." I pointed at her. "How many sixty-year-old women do you know that use the word 'party,' as a verb?" I looked at the counselor pleadingly.

My mother looked away sheepishly. Quietly, she repeated, "I like to party a little bit."

Then, my dad leaned forward in his seat and said the stupidest thing. "Wait a minute. Wait a minute. Now, go back. What did you say about Nanny?" His voice was lilting with a question mark. "Nanny . . . Nanny didn't die from alcohol. Why do you keep making up such things? Michelle, what is wrong with you? Do you hate us that much that you would make up things like that?" He looked at the counselor and shook his head with disgust.

"Are you kidding?" I yelled. "Are you kidding me? Aunt Nanny drank more than she ate or breathed. Are you kidding? She was as yellow as a banana when she died from liver failure!" I jeered. My

Aunt Nanny, once a beautiful, vivacious woman had ended up being sixty-eight pounds. Her face had shrunken so much that she could not wear her dentures. Her body was wrought with every symptom of alcoholism. It had affected her brain to such a degree that she could no longer put one foot in front of the other when she walked up steps. She was forty-six years old when she died. She was, to me, an American tragedy—a completely preventable American tragedy.

"Well," he settled back into his chair, "that's news to me. I never heard that in my life." He shook his head in bewilderment.

I was spent already and we had just begun. I rolled my eyes and shook my head. "Well, I don't know what you were doing when we had that intervention for Aunt Nanny, but I thought all that talk about alcohol and her not drinking it was about her being an alcoholic." I mocked a quizzical look. "I know, I know. I'm crazy. You're all sane as Einstein and I'm nuts. Whatever. Just thinking it might be a good thing if Mom didn't drink herself to death, that's all."

Next, I broached the subject about our kids. Aside from the drinking and driving, there was more: A few years earlier, our son Austin had come home from a weekend spent with my parents. He proceeded to have a week of vomiting night terrors. When I asked him what was causing his panic, he told us how one of my adult cousins had tormented him at a family birthday party my parents had taken him to. Without provocation, this cousin began to taunt Austin, making fun of his tidy haircut and his Christian upbringing. He verbally jabbed at him. Eventually, while ten or more people looked on—including my parents—this adult cousin began to pull at Austin's pants. It would end in my son screaming, crying, fighting off my twenty-six-year-old cousin, while he repeatedly attempted to pull down Austin's pants with absolutely no one defending him. Austin was six years old when that happened.

My dad was stymied. "I don't know anything about this," he said.

30

Of course, it was exactly as I expected from him. "I don't even know what you're talking about. Here you go making things up again." He shook his head.

This time, my mother followed suit: "I wasn't in the room when that happened," though Austin said they both were. There could be no arguing this point. Having them call my beloved son a liar through their denial would have only infuriated me even more. I knew that. Denial is a strong silencer. I had learned that from a lifetime of it.

The last thing that came from that doomed counseling session was my painful confrontation of how my parents had callously handled a horrific incident in my life. At twenty-four I had been raped. After that, I had become suicidal. At that point, I could not get out of bed. For a week I called in sick to work and cried all day in my bed, unable to function any longer.

In truth, I had been in a downward spiral after ending a physically and emotionally abusive relationship with my college boyfriend. I had broken up with him days after graduating from college. In his opinion, I was ugly, stupid, and could not even smile properly. He would pick me apart in snapshots, telling me how my smile was hideously big and my hair was never quite right. He compared me to my own friends, telling me of his secret special connections with each one. He had proceeded to tell me how he would cap his insults, someday, by eventually dating all of my friends. It was a last and final fight with him that knocked me momentarily unconscious that made me finally break up with him. He had shoved me into a wall and my head hit it hard. I blacked out and when I woke, he was furious that I had passed out. He was busily doing schoolwork, and looked over his shoulder to say to me that if I was going to be stupid and hit my head into the wall, I should leave his house. I remember thinking that being alone would be better than being with him and I was convinced that I would, indeed, be alone forever.

From my youth, my dad had essentially communicated to me the same thing. On my first date at sixteen, my dad told me the boy probably didn't call back because I hadn't let him kiss me. According to my father, if I wanted a boy to love me, I would have to give up on all my hard-edged rules, boundaries, and Debbie-Do-Gooder principles.

After my abusive relationship, I believed I was meant to be alone. I had left that relationship hating myself and set on a course of self-destructive behavior. As a girl, I had fantasized about being someone's everything. I woke up in my early twenties being nobody's anything. I had become someone I didn't even like and behaved in uncharacteristic ways, ways a healthy me would not have chosen. Being raped was simply the grand finale of my personal apocalypse.

After incessantly crying, my mother wept and cried for me to tell her what was wrong. I did, but instead of being met with love and care, my parents turned my anguish into a melodrama about themselves. My mother sobbed in my place. My dad became incensed. He told me to never mention it again. When I cried, "I don't know what to do. I don't want to live," he glared at me with a cold expression and said he'd go get me a loaded gun so I could finish it and get it over with. My mother gasped and shouted, "Jack! Don't say that," and she turned to me and soothed, "We just won't talk about it anymore. We'll just never mention it again, right?" She petted my hair and held me to her chest. Now we both had pains we couldn't acknowledge: We were finally the same. To her, I'm sure everything seemed fine. To me, I seethed with rage toward both of them.

When I confronted them about it in the counselor's office, Rick by my side, they both vehemently denied such a thing had ever taken place. In fact, my father jabbed, "She's crazy. She's always making things up." I screamed louder than my voice had ever been that I hated him and he was a pathological liar. When I finished and broke into sobs, my mother patted my knee. I had wanted an apology. Even if they had just said they didn't know what to do at the time and handled it the best they could, I would have been fine, but to deny it even happened was such a slap in the face. Also, I knew in my heart that if they could do something so callous to me, they could do as much, if not worse, to my children: That would never be an option. After that, we didn't speak for a year and a half.

Rather than tell people the truth, it was far easier for my parents to blame my faith in Christ on our separation. I think they also told people what a snob I was. There were members of my family who would have liked that. One family member even chastised me for what went on in that counseling appointment, not giving me a breath to explain or defend myself. In all honesty, it was my faith in Jesus Christ that saved me. Had I not found Jesus Christ, I would have been as worthless as they thought I was. I would have had no other choice than to adopt their opinions of me, and I would have been on the dismal path to killing myself. I knew that life had possibilities, but living in my home…well, the possibilities were hard to see sometimes.

My parents could blame my Christian faith on what separated us, and in some way, I guess they were right. It did separate us: It gave me eternal hope and it left them in a hopeless pit. Little by little, I had learned that "those who trust in themselves are fools, but those who walk in wisdom are kept safe" (Proverbs 28:26). After getting out of an abusive relationship, I had lived a life trusting in my own instincts and shortsighted wisdom and it had left me dismally void, but when I put my faith in Christ, my life was finally turned right side up—settled and stable, content and peaceful.

Eventually, God had put it on my heart to write my mom a letter pleading with her to get sober and right before God. She claimed to be a Christian, so I approached her as though she were as committed to Christ as she claimed. There was a verse I wanted her to think about that had hit me like a ton of bricks: "Not everyone who says to me, 'Lord, Lord,' will enter the kingdom of heaven, but only the one who does the will of my Father who is in heaven" (Matthew 7:21). Regardless of how my mom treated me, or acted toward me, and regardless of how she gossiped about me to anyone who would listen, I longed for her to be heaven bound.

Unabashedly, I wrote her a letter pleading with her to choose life over death because it was as though people had either forgotten, or maybe never knew how many people in our family had died from alcoholism. Aunt Nanny was the most recent death, but my mom's first cousin died before he was forty, and my mom's Uncle Olaf, my Grandpa Willard's brother, died when he was just thirty-six. He had become so dependent on alcohol that the doctors told him to carry a flask, so that when he began to shake he could soothe it with even more alcohol. For me, that letter was my last ditch plea to urge her away from the cliff. When I doubted what God was prompting me to do, He gave me this verse: "Even if I caused you sorrow by my letter, I do not regret it. Though I did regret it—I see that my letter hurt you, but only for a little while—yet now I am happy, not because you were made sorry, but because your sorrow led you to repentance. For you became sorrowful as God intended and so were not harmed in any way by us. Godly sorrow brings repentance that leads to salvation and leaves no regret, but worldly sorrow brings death" (2 Corinthians 7:8–10).

I hoped beyond all hope that my mom would live a long, beautiful life—that she would be able to defeat her demons. I hoped for her to have a life that was rich and abundant in happiness, just like I had found.

However, my mother could not let go of her past. She held onto it with the tenacity of someone clinging to a life preserver, but it wasn't a life preserver. It was the anchor and it was going down to the very bottom of the ocean. Contrary to what my dad said, at forty-six, Nanny had died from alcohol. At fifty, Bess had died from an asthma attack mixed with a sleep aid, and my grandparents had died years earlier. With one sister still alive, my mother was holding onto a past that had no future. She had always believed she was in control of nearly everything, but sometimes you lose control. Sometimes the road is unexpectedly perplexing and when you least expect it, you crash.

Chapter 3 - The Crash

I will never forget that day. It was 1:30-ish. In the middle of my day, I suddenly become strangely weighted down, as though someone had cast a heavy blanket of obsidian over me. I was in the midst of working out to a DVD when I was unable to push through the bank of fog. I threw back my white, airy duvet and crawled back into bed. For a half hour I lay on my left side, staring at the spleen of the Bible on my nightstand and wondered, Why is suicide so bad? Is it a sin? Is it? God, would you care?

Then, when the witching hour seemed to pass, I threw back the covers and went back to my workout, trying to cast off whatever gloom had momentarily come over me. It wasn't long until my kids called to me from the living room.

"Mom! Dad's on the phone! Moooom!" Austin, my oldest son handed me the phone as I patted sweat from my face with a towel.

"Hey, honey," I said, not thinking to tell him of my momentary dip into darkness. "What's up?"

He was silent, but I could hear him breathing.

"Rick?"

"Michelle, has your dad called you?"

"No . . . no. I don't think so—"

"Don't pick up his call," he interrupted. "Promise me, you won't take his call if the other line rings."

"Yeah, OK. OK, what's wrong? What's—"

"Michelle, something bad has happened, something really bad." He was out of breath, or was he laughing? Was this a joke? The other line began to ring. I ignored it, just as Rick had asked.

"Honey, are you OK? What's wrong?"

"Sweetheart, there's no other way to say it. Your mom, your—" He stumbled. He was crying. Yes, he was crying.

"What? What is it?" I pressed the phone into my ear to hear better. My heart was pounding.

"Your mom is dead. She shot herself. She's dead. She shot herself in the head." He was crying.

"What? What did you say?" I was in disbelief.

"Your mom—"

It had sunk in. "No," I said softly, and then louder, "No! No! No!" I was shouting and stomping the floor, as though my foot would crash through the floor and deeply plunge into seven layers of dirt. "No!" In the midst of my children's three stunned faces, I threw the phone and ran from our house to our neighbor's. I pounded on her door until I realized she wasn't home. I sobbed on her doorstep and realized that I had to gather myself before going back home. I had left my kids in shocked silence. As I trudged slowly back across the lawn, I saw their sweet faces pressed against the window, looking for me. My God, help me, I thought. Give me the words to say.

I went into the house to find them wondering if Rick was OK. "He's fine," I soothed. "Daddy's fine. He'll be home in a little bit. Everything's OK. I just heard some shocking news, that's all." I wiped away tears, trying to appear normal. "I don't want to talk about it right now, though. I'm sorry I reacted that way. I'm sorry." I patted their heads and kissed them. "I'm going to go outside for a while. You guys just stay in here, OK? Watch something on TV, 'K?"

They could not hide their fear. Their furrowed brows followed me as I gently closed the door behind me. To this day, they still do not know how my mother died. I still cannot bear to tell them. I cannot bear their sorrow.

I sat on the porch, hung my head, and sobbed. My mom was dead. I fought the temptation to call her, to dial her cell number—a number I could easily dial in my sleep—just so she could tell me that everyone was wrong, just so she could say it was all a misunderstanding. Yes, I wanted my mom to tell me that everything would be OK. No matter how bad our relationship had gotten, she could be the most soothing person when I desperately needed her to be soothing, but her soft words and gentle ways would never come again. I was just an hour away from being able to hear her tell me it would be OK. I had called her the night before, but she hadn't called me back. I had waited for her call. I had been sure she'd call, eventually. Regarding time, nothing but a miniscule fraction separated us; regarding life, we were indelibly separated by death. I sat wishing I were next to her, wherever she was, so I could grasp at her last breath as it soared into the atmosphere. It was time to get on and grow up. No more. No more Mom. No more hoping for a happy ending. No more.

The day after her suicide—after we'd gotten my best friend to care for our children—Rick and I drove to Dayton, Nevada, to convene with other relatives at my uncle's house. That is what normal families tend to do, I suppose, though "normal" is not exactly how I would categorize some members of my family. When the dust settled, I found that after three days of drinking my mom had curled up on her left side in her bed, took her .22-caliber, pink-handled revolver my father bought her for "protection," put it to her right temple, and pulled the trigger. She was dead in an instant.

On the long, seven-hour, stormy November drive to that desolate little Nevada town, I remembered a conversation I'd had with my mom, wherein I asked her why she needed a gun in her purse, or on the headboard of her bed, or worse and certainly most alarming, under her pillow.

"Are people breaking into houses? Are there packs of wild dogs attacking people?" I mean, she lived in Nevada—anything was possible.

"Uh . . . no, no," she stammered. "Your dad just thinks it's safer."

"Hmm. Safer?" I questioned. "Safer than what?" She was an alcoholic. I could not conceive how my mother cradling a gun in her various inebriated states was ever going to be safe. Just a few years earlier, she had undergone a gastric bypass surgery. Having long been addicted to alcohol, shopping, and gambling, she had found what she believed to be at least an answer for her food addiction. With the cutting-edge procedure, she quickly lost one hundred pounds; however, the procedure never prepared her for those other addictions, particularly her alcoholism. With her digestive system rearranged, alcohol consumption made her an entirely different person. She simply could not process and manage it, as she once had. Mentally and emotionally, she was someone else.

She had already told me that one night she had hallucinated about hearing her long dead sister, Nanny, call to her from the kitchen. She had gotten out of bed and followed the voice, finally awakening enough to realize that there was no one there and coming back to the cold reality that Nanny had been dead from alcoholism for almost twenty years. My dad, however, thought otherwise and encouraged my mother to sign up for a concealed weapons license, insisting she carry her gun with her at all times, even in her purse. It was so typical of my dad to instill an overwhelming sense of fear.

When I lived alone in college, I too was given a gun and was told incessantly about the dangers, fears, and boogeyman that awaited me around every corner. Though nothing ever happened to me, fear controlled my every thought. I knew why my mother had given into carrying a gun in her purse. I'm sure every sensational newspaper headline was depicted as though it were only dumb luck that she had escaped it. I understood that with enough coaxing and terrifying regurgitations of violent crimes, she had come to believe that something frightful might occur if she was not prepared; and yet, the most frightful presence was the one who had cozied snugly next to her, feigning care and concern.

By his own account, my dad recounted how he had the faculty, upon finding my mother's dead body, to call not only the police but an attorney prior to allowing investigators into their home. You see, he was building an illegal AK-47 automatic assault rifle in his garage, and he was clearheaded enough to know that it was a felony. With my mother's body still warm in her bed and the gun slightly amiss next to her pretty face, he pulled out a phone book and began dialing for some narcissistic coverage. "Protect thyself," must surely have been what his inner demon was screaming out, and protect himself he did.

The dial-an-attorney told him he would have to allow police inside, so when they came he proceeded to pour out the most melodramatic dribble the police had ever seen. "Oh, my wife! My baby! My wife, my wife! My baby!" How is it that no one saw this sort of emotional outpouring before he called the attorney? Well, no matter, because it worked, and the police, feeling sorry for him, took his homemade AK-47 and let him off with just a warning.

But his melodrama continued, as he settled in with my uncle in the days following my mother's death. With each new mourner's arrival, tearlessly he would reach for an old picture of my mother and show each person, saying, "Wasn't she beautiful? Wasn't she perfect? Oh, my wife! My baby! My wife, my wife! My baby!" (This is about the closest I can get to the exact verbiage he repetitively used). After a second or third round of caterwauling, he would settle and talk in his normal tone and voice, as though the first stint of melodrama was exactly that, melodrama. In fact, it got a little tiring for him after a while, so when about the eleventh person came to pay their respects, it began to get a little sloppy and it was more like: "Oh, my wife! My baby! My wife, my wife!" He grabbed the picture, poked it in their face and continued, "Wasn't she beautiful? Hey, is that clam dip over there? Can I get some of that on a plate with some crackers? Yeah, and I wouldn't mind a beer either."

In some sick way, my dad seemed pleased to have an audience. He had never been anyone's favorite. Especially when my gregarious, fun-loving mother was around.

"I told your mom, I told her," he leaned on me, "don't get too drunk or you won't be able to tell the police how to get to the house."

I turned my face to him, looking at him quizzically. "Why was there talk of police? How did the police get brought into the conversation?"

"Well, you know your mom." He shrugged, absentmindedly. "She and I were arguing over the phone . . ." He faded off, looking at her picture and trying hard to cry. He did not want to explain why he would allude to the police, but in my heart, I knew. My dad had already revealed that he and my mother had been in a dispute on the telephone when she killed herself. He worked in the San Francisco Bay Area during the week and went home to my mother in Carson City, Nevada, on the weekends. He had been on his way home when she called to tell him their house was in foreclosure, and obviously a quarrel had ensued. In truth, the foreclosure proceedings had gone so far and she had withheld so much, they only had sixty days left before they were to be evicted. I knew their finances, which my mother had always juggled like flaming wands, were in a crisis.

They had moved to a brand new house in a dusty little Nevada suburb and tried to "retire," but their extravagant expenditures would not conform to my father's retirement standards. No, you could not rebuild a muscle car, or have all the latest guns and off-road vehicles in an unplanned retirement, so they were in the process of losing their home: For a couple who prided themselves on parading their possessions in front of friends, relatives, and neighbors, it was a tough pill to swallow.

What I believed, but will never know for certain, is that when my mother got to her wits' end this time and threatened to kill herself— as she often did—my father did nothing to dissuade her. In fact, I wondered if he had given her the same loving response he gave me years earlier when I struggled with reasons to stay alive in the aftermath of being raped. Had she finally gotten her fill of forty-six years of physical, mental, and emotional abuse? What else could explain his comments to her about being too drunk to direct the police to their home? Had he miscalculated? Had he believed that she would pop some pills and then, with great regret, call police and emergency vehicles to their home at the last minute? I don't know. I'll never know for sure, but I have my guesses and it's all speculation as to why that statement was made. I know that the affairs my father had with my mother's so-called friends made her sick to her stomach and the one he'd had with her best friend had been a knife to her heart. She had called me months earlier to tell me.

It was nighttime and she was drunk, as she always was by nightfall. My dad was not home. It was a weekday and he was in California for work. As usual she was slurring and blithering on about her deep disappointments. She talked sorrowfully about her dead sisters. I let her cry. She missed them. Then, she said, "You know, Shelly, I know a lot of things, too many things, 'bout your dad and Cindy. If you knew what I know, you'd never forgive either of them." She began to cry. "It's awful . . . jus' awful." My mom already told me about her suspicions of my father's infidelities. She had kept me informed throughout my entire life telling me things a child shouldn't know. I had always worked with focused diligence to avoid it, because to me it was just another secret, just another thing to hide. I soothed her. I told her if she wanted to leave him, I'd be there. "It's OK," she said. "I've stayed this long." She had said that countless times before. I thought it was such a hopeless thing to say, such a dismally hopeless thing, but she was immovable. I knew the decision had to be hers.

The fact that my parents had been married for forty-six years meant nothing to me; it was an affront to marriage. My mother had always wanted quantity to misplace quality. I could see that. Her own parents were a smattering of haphazard parts that came together by my mother's illegitimate birth. Eventually, my grandparents ended up together, but marital bliss was sporadic. My grandfather would only mellow as age calmed his wild ways. For me, he was a funny and outgoing grandpa, but since my mother's death, I have thought there were probably only three or four decent years of normalcy in my mother's childhood home before she met and married my father at the age of eighteen.

Yes, my mom was determined to make her marriage work, or at best, make it look as though it worked. For all the fantasy she had spun out of misery, she could have written romance novels. Though I had begged her for years to leave my dad, she was committed to staying. It did not matter how my father treated her. She would not leave. At some point, I ceased to care what she did because I realized in my teenage years that you cannot make anyone do anything they are not bound and determined to do. You cannot want for someone what they will not choose for themselves.

Though they could have fought over my father's infidelities, my parents usually fought over skewed finances. My father especially had no respect for the practical side of finances. My entire life, he had insisted that money be there—just magically be there in an imaginary treasure chest in our backyard when he wanted it, lest his temper explode and he beat my mother for the lack thereof. It would all begin just as routinely as clockwork. "There's no money? There's no money? How could there be no money? I work too damned hard for there to be no money," he'd begin, punching the wall or hitting his fist hard against the table.

"And," he'd taunt my overly drawn-out mother, "you…you don't even know work," even though my mother was as fine as any single mother, committed to working full-time and taking care of all the child-rearing responsibilities. Going above and beyond, my mother had even been a Little League umpire for my brother and had taken baton lessons with me, so I might learn my routines better. My father worked nights until I was sixteen years old, so he wasn't even a rare sight at our dinner table. He was more like a ghostly apparition who bullied us when sacrifices weren't made properly at his rocky shrine. Not only was I afraid of him, I learned to despise his presence.

Back at my uncle's house, my mind was still trying to grasp the reality of my mom's suicide. Grief had taken down the walls I'd built against my father. As I sat next to him he grabbed my hand and fumbled with my fingers. "Your hands … they're so like your mother's." They are nothing alike, I thought. "I'll never forget seeing your mom's pretty fingers right there," he said, toying with my fingers until they were in the position of holding the trigger of a gun, "right on the trigger." I quickly pulled back my hands and dug them deeply into my lap.

"Now, Shelly, I made arrangements for us to go see her in the morgue. We'll all go. Your brother Keith, you, and me."

"The morgue? Yeah," I shook my head gently, "I'm not doing that."

"Oh yeah, you are. Of course you are. It'll be good for you to see her." Images of deer hunting trips flashed through my head, of half-skinned deer hanging from high branches of stark, leafless trees. When my father would get a deer, he would skin the deer to the neck, leaving the head intact, with legs cut off at the joints, skinned—tendons, muscles, veins, and vessels exposed. It was gruesome, but it was his trophy. One year a mountain lion attacked a bagged deer in the middle of the night. In the morning, it was nothing more than bloody shreds of meat, dangling from a gray, stiff branch.

No, no, no. I would not see this trophy. I would not give my father the satisfaction of acknowledging his greatest triumph. Never. Never, ever. My mother would never reside in my brain as something he had conquered.

"In the morgue?" I asked again. "No, not going to do that. I don't need to see her like that," I said. It was as though Satan had looked for the hook, the thing to drive me insane, and he had found it with this. My father prodded mercilessly to get me to his home, the place where my mother had ended her life. It seemed as though he wanted me to see the carnage—the blood splattered wall of their bedroom that I had glazed a pretty lavender for her two years prior, the blood-soaked mattress. The mere idea of such things was driving me mad. Yes, by reason of my father's insanity, I was going mad.

"You should see it," he said. "It's really not that bad. I think a little cleaning and it won't even show." He paused, appearing to gather his thoughts. "I just wish she hadn't used that gun . . ." He faded off.

I cringed. My mind entertained that last line. What gun had she used? I assumed she used her small .22-caliber, but with those words, I struggled to think that my mom could have used the .44 magnum. In layman's terms, think of it this way. If a .44 is double the size of the .22, it does double the damage. Yes, both had the same overall result, but the latter would make my dad's insistence on seeing my mother in the morgue even more grotesque, more macabre, and thoroughly sinister. I was breathing heavily, trying to absorb the idea. It was as if someone had thrown a hammer smack dab in the middle of my brain. I felt as though I was beginning to shut down. My own thoughts were becoming unwelcome adversaries.

"Yeah, not that bad," he continued and patted me on the back. "It won't take too long to clean up." I knew he had found in me just the person to tidy up. I tried to remain civil in light of the fact that my mother had just killed herself, but inside my mind was racing.

"No, no, Dad. I'm not doing that. I'm not going there ever." That word, the word "ever" was like a crumb, a scrap, a taunt, and a challenge. He would never let go of the goal of getting me to his home, and I felt certain with his ever incessant nudging that Satan lurked there, awaiting my arrival, so that I would indeed go completely insane, collapsing under the weight of his demonic attack against me, like an outpaced gazelle finally succumbing to a cheetah.

Two of my friends had told me before I left for Nevada that God impressed on them for me not to go to my parents' home. One friend had cried, saying, "I don't know why, but I know if you go there it will be bad. It will be horrible. Please, promise me you won't go there."

I promised her because I felt it too. Whatever lurked there, waiting for me, would not be satiated until it devoured my mother and me in a near simultaneous attack. No, I would never ever go there—ever. I felt certain I would not exit that home alive and I was enormously terrified by the thought.

In fact, Rick and I had already driven seven hours through a blizzard with no delusions of even spending one full night in that town or general vicinity. No, we would spend as little time in this spiritually dark place as possible. Because you see, regardless of my parents' initial excitement to move from California to Nevada, I had always felt a morose unease in this place, as though a perpetual dark cloud loomed all about, even on glaringly sunny days. From the toothless meth tweakers roaming aimlessly through the aisles of the local Wal-Mart to the openly advertised brothels, this place was overwhelmingly dark—a spiritually bleak landscape best compared to Mars, without the excitement of the Mars' Rover cruising by and snapping photos of rocks.

When my parents first moved to this Nevada city I had cried for hours. Years before my mother's untimely death, I could not even explain my deep sadness, though I kept saying to Rick, "It's over. I just know it's over forever." I know now that my spiritual discernment was trying to tell me what my head did not want to acknowledge. My mother had decided with resolute determination to take a turn into a dark tunnel that led directly to an oncoming locomotive. It was, indeed, over.

My father continued, "Well, I have to take a shower and I need laundry done. Baby," he cooed softly. He was using the exact words he used regularly with my mother. "Baby, just come home with me. There are things that need to be washed."

I envisioned my father handing me bloodied bed sheets to wash, my hands mingling with sudsy water and my own mother's blood. For sure, I was going crazy. I felt as though my head were in a vice, squeezing, squeezing, clamping down harder and harder.

"So," he said, suddenly changing the subject, "I figured out that I'll get at least $250,000 in life insurance. I'll be able to buy a new truck and a new motorhome. I'll sell your mom's car—"

"Dad," I interrupted softly, "I don't think you get insurance money from a suicide." I was embarrassed that he would talk of such a thing so soon. Like the lies our little family had always kept, I spoke in a whisper, so no one would hear. I was ashamed of him for the thousandth time in my life.

"No," he responded, "I already checked, and I'll get it. Now I know why your mom did it." I dreaded to hear his justification. "She did it so I could keep all my stuff. She did it for me. She knew . . . she knew I'd get to keep all my stuff. My baby did this for me, but it's not worth it. It's not. Oh, my wife! My baby! My wife."

He quickly settled down when he realized no one was watching him anymore. "So, Shelly, what do you think? Why don't we just run over to the house, so I can take a shower and you can run a load of laundry for me?"

"No, no, I won't go there," I protested, shaking my head. At that moment, Rick came back, taking me and leading me away.

"Jack," he defended, "she doesn't want to go there, and she never will." Thank God for the strength of a good, godly man.

I tried settling in among my other family members, but my cousin Alex continued to glare at me with inflamed rage in his eyes. He had already met my husband and me in the middle of the street when we pulled up. Before I could even reach the sidewalk, he had approached me with his head bowed.

"Don't feel guilty. Don't feel guilty. She loved you," Alex had said, as if there were outstanding verdicts on both. When I didn't respond, he repeated, "Yeah, really, don't feel guil—"

"I don't," I interrupted. "Why would I?"

He shrugged. "No reason, I guess."

When I sat near Alex on a deep mahogany leather sofa in the living room, he wrenched himself upward in a huff to leave the room abruptly and glare at me from a greater distance. We had once been so close. I had hoped with our shared grief, we would be close again, but when I ignorantly settled near him again on the floor of another room, I began to get the third degree from him.

"Sooooo," he hissed quietly, glancing quickly over my shoulder to make sure Rick would not hear and come to my defense, "what was your relationship like with your mom?"

"It was OK, I guess."

"Humph," he huffed. "Really?" The word was coated in sarcasm.

"It was as good as it could be, considering."

"Considering what?" Alex demanded, his eyes narrowing at me.

"Considering she was an alcoholic," I said matter-of-factly.

He shook his head mockingly, smiling a crooked smile, as if to say, "You just don't get it, do you?"

But, I got it and I thought, 'Well, here we go.' Surely my mother's relationship and mine had not been what it had once been and it was not what I longed for; however, contrary to what some people believed, it had gotten better the six months prior to her death. God had given me that, prompting me to let go of anything in our way and accept my mother for who she was. Yes, that was wholly and entirely on God's leading, since for me, my mother's alcoholism had been the reason for our broken relationship. When she was inebriated, she could unleash the meanest attacks on me, telling me she would not even hurt or cry if I died, telling me she would never care for me the way she did her sisters, flaunting the exclusivity that had been ours with marginal relationships that would endorse her self-destruction, and making sure that I knew I was nothing to her. Contrary to what many people thought, I had endured far more than they knew—things for which they only saw my anger, not the preceding offenses.

I had continued to pull in the boundaries of my play yard until it could no longer accommodate any play at all. At last, I packed up the play yard and put it away. There were no more options. It was with the greatest regret that I found myself at odds with my mother. I never wanted to be on the opposite side of the fence from her, for I knew that it would mean a slow, painful death to many of my relationships with family. As the family matriarch, her influence would relegate me to the status of hated malcontent. As evidence of her attempts to blackball me, I would later find out that she tracked down one of my former junior high classmate's mothers who had long moved to another city. Though my mother had never once socialized with this woman, she sought her out for the sole purpose of telling her what a horrible daughter I'd become.

In truth, it is exactly what I expected. I even told my mom that I knew distancing myself from her would be like trying to leave a cult. Everyone would ostracize me forever. Frankly, I could have endured what had become customary, but for my children, I was intent on protecting my babies, so that nothing else mattered, not even the ridicule, rejection, and constant ill assessment from those who thought they knew better. No, compared to my children, all these people, all the people judging me based on gossip rather than fact, were nothing more than sand pouring away into the wind and I would choose my children every time.

From the pointed questioning, Alex began, "Well, I know I wouldn't mind taking her car. We'll have to see about her jewelry." He was intent on putting me in my place. I didn't want to tell him that my father had already told me he'd be selling her car. Let them work out those details. I allowed time to settle around us like dust shaken from a rug. Finally, through all the shock, it was emerging that somehow, to all these people gathered at my uncle's house, I was to blame. I could feel it.

"Alex," I said, breaking the permeation of hatred. "Can we go outside and talk?" He nodded.

We stood outside on the porch of my uncle's house, letting the crisp November air wrap around us. Bright stars twinkled in a velvet sky. "What's going on here?" I asked. "It seems like everyone is blaming me . . . maybe without saying it outright, but saying it anyway. What's up?"

He shook his head and smiled. "Look," he said, "Everyone knows what your relationship was with your Mom. Everyone knows…"

"Do they? Do they know that she and I talked two or three times a week and she just wrote me an e-mail saying I was such an encouragement to her? Does everyone know that? Do they know that we were supposed to spend Christmas together? Do they?"

He was silent. Alex had always been quick to provide my mother alternative social opportunities for drinking when I tried to shut them down. I had found that an intervention of one is like trying to stop an incoming tsunami by throwing sand at it.

"No, everyone doesn't know everything, and I'm not to blame because she killed herself. I think her alcohol was to blame for that." The Holy Spirit stopped me here because for years my family and my father had seemingly worked against me to confront my mother's alcoholism. I could understand that. Anyone who confronted her about her alcoholism would need to be prepared for a hailstorm of backlash.

He scowled at me. "No, no, it wasn't alcohol. Don't say that!" he stammered. "It was you." He began to cry.

"Alex," I said as I softened, "I know I could say a lot right now—

equally hurtful things—but the Holy Spirit is telling me not to. Miraculously, the Holy Spirit is shutting my mouth against you." And it was a miracle because my big mouth had gotten loose and run rampant on more than one occasion, but this night, this night when God knew that I needed to remain silent, the Holy Spirit stood firmly with His hand over my mouth.

"It was . . . it was you. She said things about you. She said . . . lots of things." He was crying in pain—brokenhearted and wounded. We were all brokenhearted and wounded.

"Did she leave a note saying it was me?" I was genuinely interested, knowing it would be hard to accept.

"No, but . . ." he defended. "There were letters on her bed. Letters from you. Two birthday cards and that letter."

"Are you talking about the letter I wrote her over a year ago? That one?" He nodded. I knew that letter—asking my mom to make a choice to get better—would never be understood by my family. I did not care. That letter was between God, my mother, and me—no one else. I felt the Holy Spirit closing my mouth and encouraging me to see my cousin through His eyes.

"Everyone knows it's your fault . . . everyone! We all know it's your fault."

"Alex, I'll say it again, the Holy Spirit is shutting my mouth to you." Saying this to him this last time was a catalyst for something I could not see. He began to stammer, until he finally relapsed into a gush of tears and ran inside the house, telling everyone inside that I had been accusing him of being the reason my mother killed herself. In fact, months later, I would hear from a relative that he turned our conversation completely around, saying that my words were his and his were mine. It was a supernatural fracas that completely upturned the events of that evening.

Rick and I left shortly after that, after just a few short hours of being glared at and being told in hushed confrontational tones that my mother's best things had already been picked over by my cousin and quasi relatives. It was fine, though. Before we had arrived, I'd already decided that I would take nothing. Anything taken from my mother's tomb would be dirty. The things that could not bring her joy or comfort would certainly be hollow to me. Let the dogs fight over it, I thought. Shortly after getting back across the California border, I vomited, as though my body was fighting off things I could not see.

Chapter 4 - The Wrecking Yard

It had been three days since my mother committed suicide. She killed herself right before Thanksgiving. With the holiday, it would be another week before her real funeral in the Bay Area with longtime family and friends. My dad, however, conducted some sort of slapdash, horrid, funerary display without me in Carson City. Without that, he might not have garnered the sympathy from all the women my mom had befriended and would have lost the opportunity to hit on them. In the midst of a stack of sympathy cards he later handed me to deal with, I found a sketchy letter from one of my mother's so-called friends. In loopy swirls, she told my father she thought of him every day. I wanted to pound that woman's face into the ground—an "asphalt facial," as I liked to call it—and lose my father under an avalanche of rubble. My simmering pot was beginning to pop with whirling bubbles, erupting into the atmosphere from a gradual boil.

To me, it looked as though my dad was quickly getting used to being center stage, even if for something ghastly and appalling. He had tried to arrange this first funeral to fall on my birthday, December 3, but, fortunately, that did not work out. Without any consideration for my mother, Keith, or me, my dad insisted my mom be cremated, even though my mother had always talked about being buried near her parents and sisters. Even with cremation, he still managed to find a way to have a public viewing of her ravaged body. I was told she was laid out on some sort of cart. He had gone as cheaply as he could, spending as little of his $250,000 insurance money as possible.

Alex called me to ask what I wanted my mom to wear, even though I would not be present. I envisioned my mother in pink. "Yes, pink," I said. I would find out later that she had been wearing pink the day she died.

I tried to describe to Alex the exact pink blouse I wanted her to wear. It was silk and had pleating down the front. My mom looked beautiful in pink. She would get so tanned that her steel-blue eyes would gleam in blossomy pink. Alex called back twenty minutes later to tell me that my mother's neck and face were too mangled to wear that blouse. They would have to opt for a turtleneck.

"Then, why did you ask in the first place?" I inquired. He had no answer. Turtlenecks were fine. My mother was used to wearing turtlenecks. She had a slew of them to cover the marks on her neck when my dad would choke her. Yeah, I'm sure a turtleneck would be fine.

I had just attempted to eke out an obituary, but with no sleep, everything was difficult. At that point, I had been awake for ninety-six hours. I didn't plan on it, but sleep was a foreign concept meant for normal people.

It was 3:12 a.m., and I was cruising the web for my mother's employer, hunting for the man who had, according to my dad, made my mom commit suicide. You see, in the heat of our grief, my shrewd, self-preserving dad had sent each member of my family on the proverbial goose chase. It was easy to send hounds in my direction, since so many family members already hated me, a homeschooling Christian who had the audacity to be the first one in the family to run off and get a college degree. Then, what stupid girl thing did I do with my haughty, snotty degree? I stayed home and homeschooled my kids! Holy crap, who did I think I was? Miss High and Mighty! Yes, there was so much to hate. But, obviously, my dad couldn't send me in that same direction—heavens no! He sent me gunning for my mother's boss, another religious freak, telling me that he had hounded my poor mother about nonsensical things until she killed herself.

Don't you worry, Mom. I'll get this Mormon jack-wad, I thought, as I tapped the keyboard. Had I been less emotional and more sober-minded, I would have known what my dad was doing. I would have known that he was tossing blame carelessly upward toward the spinning blades of a ceiling fan and hoping they would land anywhere but near him.

In truth, there was a part of me that was simply hoping that someone, something, some specific reasonable incident had pushed my mother to kill herself. I needed to believe that she ended her life based upon some extraordinarily dire circumstance, not something trivial and meaningless, like the materialistic contentment and mollification of my father, or worse, me. I wanted to believe that her boss, Doug, was truly horrible, cruel, and ruthless. Had I believed anything else, my feelings of loss would have been unbearable in those first few days.

It was on the fourth sleepless night after her death that I hunted for Doug. "Doug, Doug, Doug, where are you Doug?" It didn't take me long to find Doug's name, then Doug's home telephone number, and eventually Doug's home address. It is pretty frightening what you can find on the Internet. "Oh, Doug, it is a very good thing we are separated by seven hours and a snowstorm."

It was now 3:24 a.m., and I dialed his number. The groggy voice of a woman answered. I hung up. My body was shaking. I hate you, Doug. My teeth chattered, as though I were freezing. I hate you, stupid Doug's wife. I dialed the number again. She answered again, and again I

56

hung up, crying like a psycho stalking the president. "I hate you. I want my mom. Why didn't you like her? Everybody liked her. Everybody!" I said this although I knew it was a lie and that my mom could make enemies out of anyone who disagreed with her, including me. I dialed the number again and this time it went into voicemail. I hung up before it could catch my heavy breathing.

I began pounding out the angriest e-mail to Doug anyone had ever written. I copied everyone in that business on it, coworkers, bosses, administrators, window washers, and janitors. I told Doug what he'd taken from me. I told him what a jerk he was, and because it was pretty scathing, I left out any obscenities. This whole Christian thing was seriously hindering me from being completely rancid, and I desperately longed to be rancid. I had held it in when accused by my family, but I deeply longed to punch someone in the face. I longed to punch Doug in the face. I knew, in my heart, that my feelings alone were wholly and entirely un-Christian. "Blaaaaach!" I hit the key to send the e-mail to countless people. I hope you choke on a caffeine loaded soda, Doug!

Admittedly, before this tragedy, I had struggled with anger. Being raised in a physically abusive home, I found anger my first stop for any negative emotions—fear, abandonment, sorrow, hurt—yes, they were all reasons to be angry, but I was trying so hard to overcome this burden, this sin, this plague of my past. Now, with my mother's horrible death, I was wallowing once again in the anger puddle. I was the woolly mammoth thrashing about in the La Brea Tar Pits and, honestly, I wasn't entirely certain I would ever make it out.

On Monday, I knew Doug had gotten my e-mail. I had angrily instructed them to remove my mother's name from their website, and by 10:37 a.m. (breakneck timing), it was removed. I wondered how many confounded people had to convene to figure that out. My rancor for all of them and the entire putrid state of Nevada swelled, like a festering boil. I had come to hate, hate, hate Nevada. I viewed it as a giant volcano that had swallowed my mommy whole.

Then, with equal determination, I began calling the Coroner's Office. I asked for, and was initially denied, the autopsy, toxicology, and police reports. However, I knew that "no" was just a word, and with enough persistence "no" could become "yes." I finally got a name and that name became my friend. I called her relentlessly. I told her every sordid detail and my reasons for needing those reports.

"Don't you see," I pleaded, "when a loved one dies, you can say things like 'she died of pancreatic cancer,' or 'it was the widow-maker.' Everyone gets to know how their loved one died. They talk to doctors and they know. I need to know what it was like when my mom died. I loved her. I have to know it wasn't because of me." And that was the truth. Even though I wanted to believe my dad was simply a jerk, I still needed to know it wasn't me that made her put a gun to her head and end her life. Reason can only get you so far, and then you want it on paper. Well, if my friend at the Coroner's Office thought I might relent, she must have eventually realized she was wrong.

I also kept e-mailing Doug. I poked at that man. Sometimes I just e-mailed to say that I wasn't going away. I also called his wife again, in the daytime. I told her who I was this time: "This is Michelle, Lena's daughter, and you can tell your husband I called." I'm sure I sounded certifiably crazy with a capital K. My voice was low and determined. In telling his wife my name, I wanted him to be haunted by the idea that some vengeful part of my mother lived on. Like Jason in Friday the 13th who was stabbed, drowned, and killed a million ways, but never died, I wanted Doug to fear me: I wanted him to be afraid I might pop up in the produce aisle of the supermarket, at the carwash, the barbershop, the shower! I wanted him to be afraid like I was afraid, afraid that my mom had taken her own life.

It enraged me to find that Doug's wife had the softest, kindest voice. I hated her stupid voice. Go bake a pie, I thought. In my mind,

Mormons did stuff like pie baking, picnicking, horseback-riding, quilt-making, and other good, wholesome stuff like that. For no reason, it made me cry. I called Doug's local Mormon temple and left a voicemail, explaining that Doug had taken undue pleasure in harassing my mother until she finally killed herself. That was about the most uncomfortable voicemail message I have ever left anywhere. I wondered what the looks on the faces of the recipients would be. Who cared? Be shocked, I thought. Be shocked like my life has been shocked—BE SHOCKED!

In the midst of all of my incessant stalking, I called my friend at the Coroner's Office again, only to be denied again. Still, I wished my friend there a nice day. Having just returned from a smoke break, her gravelly voice apologized for not being able to send me the reports.

"It's OK, Gloria," I said. "Thanks for trying. I'm sure I don't need to say it, but I'll talk to you tomorrow."

She let out a raspy laugh. "Well, tomorrow's Saturday. We won't be here."

"It doesn't matter," I said. "I'll call anyway."

"I know you will," she chuckled again, "I know you will."

I knew I was losing it. In an effort to curb my craziness, I sent an e-mail to a Care Pastor at church. With all the outrageous behavior I was unleashing on the entire state of Nevada, I was pretty sure it was only a matter of time before someone knocked on my door with either handcuffs or a straightjacket. In truth, I would have required both and maybe a K9 unit too.

I had never had problems of this magnitude before, so contacting the church about my mountainous set of problems was also new. I had never wanted to be one of those people. We churchies all know who those people are. They are the ones that no matter what is going on, it's all doom and gloom. They are incessantly embroiled in one crisis and then another. It never ever ends. Those people are the ones who are always engulfed in some sort of high-drama. They are frankly the people everyone tries to avoid because no matter how much money you give them, or what advice, they never get better. At some point, it becomes generational.

No, I did not want to be like that, nor did I want others to treat me as if I were one of those people. No, I had become like all good but jaded church-goers; I never had problems and that is exactly how I wanted to keep it. Unfortunately, the truth of the matter was that life was kicking my tail up and down the street, and I believed that I was just two tail kicks away from losing my mind. I needed help.

So, out of sheer desperation I sent the church's Care Pastor a message asking for help. My message to him was simple: "My mother killed herself. My husband and I are in a desperate lawsuit. I am struggling. Please help me."

Oh yes, the lawsuit. In spite of my opposition and protests, Rick and I had purchased an integrated circuit business from a self-professed Christian man and his wife. While she had probably once been arm candy, she was now in her late seventies, and according to the man, she was dying. He needed someone reliable, honest, trustworthy, and preferably Christian to take his business off his hands for a mere million dollars. While he could have sold his business to a gaggle of beggars, he kindly and generously thought Rick was the most deserving—the one and only candidate worthy enough.

Strangely, though, I did not consider the man to possess any of those admirable qualities. In fact, I observed that after he invited us to an expensive restaurant to lull us into his snare, he treated the staff with contempt and pretended not to see the check when it came. Instead, he waited for Rick to pick up the bill, while he pretended not to see that transaction out of the corner of his eye. I thought he was a louse, but Rick was vehemently convinced that we could overtake him in cunning and believed in his heart that the old man would eventually ride away into the sunset on a gold-plated golf cart after we purchased the business. Well, neither of those things happened. That old man was more cunning than a fox, and he wouldn't go away until he ruined us completely.

After he sold us the business with nothing to sell (his vendors had canceled him just twelve days prior to our contract signing), he sexually harassed one of our young employees, and began to ruin our reputations wherever and whenever he could. Not only that, he prompted our competitors to steal anything that was salvageable, all while taking a salary and continuing to collect on the personal loan we had taken with him in order to buy his dead business.

Needless to say, we ended up in a lawsuit. All I know from the legal system is that it doesn't much matter who is right or wrong, it only matters who has more money because the one with the most money wins. This is why in one meeting with this creeper and his attorney, he could tell us that he would ruin us down to our children and mean it. Getting furious and threatening to dangle him out of the sixth floor window where we were meeting was answered with the fact that security guards would come for me.

"Yeah," I said with a maniacal laugh, "well, I've seen those ol' tired security guards and it'll take at least ten minutes for them to taze me. I can do plenty of damage in ten minutes." I stood and leaned across the table and emphasized, "Never, ever mention my children again!"

The creeper would not mention our children again. Instead, he would drive by our house at all hours because he had told us that he would relish the day that we were depleted of all our money, evicted, and kicked out of our home. I envisioned him taunting our kids as their bikes and beds were sold at a garage sale, for that was the kind of man we were dealing with: evil, purely evil.

Naively, our strategy was to be truthful in court. More astutely, his strategy was to run us out of money. His strategy is more widely accepted and successful. Idiots who think the truth will set you free in a court of law need to avoid situations where they might end up in a court of law. Be warned, the truth and the law have nothing in common.

Anyway, sending an e-mail to the Care Pastor, I thought the time at which I sent it said as much as the message itself: I sent it at 1:43 a.m. Saturday night, or rather Sunday morning. At that same time, I called the Coroner's Office, just as I told Gloria I would. I left a tearful voicemail. Obviously, they were closed, but I called two more times that weekend to leave a recorded message. I begged for the reports, explaining that I did not know how to get on with my life until I had them. That following Monday, I received a return call from Gloria. She let me know that in a sad turn of events, the Deputy Coroner who had been holding up the release of the reports had unexpectedly died that weekend. She mailed out the reports to me that morning, which I received the following Wednesday.

Initially, I tried to wait until Rick got home to open the large manila envelope. When I could wait no longer, I went to our bedroom, locked the door, and ripped the tab open. I devoured those reports. My father had been much more forthcoming with the six police officers who were on the scene than with our family. He told them he knew my mother was on antidepressants, Vicodin, and numerous other pain medications. He knew she was an alcoholic, though he told every one of my family members that she was completely sober the day she killed herself. In fact, the story would dwindle down to the miniscule point that she was sober enough to be so utterly and fully heartbroken by me that she saw no other alternative but to kill herself. However, in the police reports, my dad went on to confess that he knew my mom had been in bed for three days intoxicated and overly medicated with prescription drugs, largely because of their dire financial problems. The report would convey that there were five empty bottles of prescription medications lying next to my mother's body, along with a scrawled message, saying she had been fired by "Dave." She could not even recall Doug's name, and she could not recall that Doug had not fired her, but instead had his assistant call her to see why she hadn't shown up for work three days in a row. The toxicology report noted that she had a .264 blood alcohol level—two and a half times the legal limit. They did not test for barbiturates or any of her prescription medications, since the cause of death was obvious.

Other notable things: Unlike my father had insinuated, my mom had used the .22 caliber hand gun, not the .44 magnum. There was one single bullet entry on the right side of her temple and no exit wound. It was nearly in her hairline. There was no reason she would have had neck lesions or damage to any other part of her body, as my dad indicated when I wanted her to wear her pink silk blouse. My mom had curled up in her bed wearing a loose pink nightshirt, and was lying on her left. She actually used her thumb, rather than her index finger to pull the trigger. There were no cards or letters on the bed, as Alex had told me, and as I'm sure my father had told him. There were just empty pill bottles and a light cotton sheet that covered my mom's curled up legs. The back sliding glass door was slightly ajar and the dog was outside.

Notably, my father's call to an attorney and the police removal of his AK-47 was not on any page of the police report. Because I am my mother's daughter, I called the reporting officer, explained who I was, and asked why he hadn't put that in his report. Barney Fife, that's what I called him, seemed confused as to how I got his telephone number and could not understand why I called him. I explained to Barney that after watching my mom get beaten up for forty-two years of my life by a horrible man, I would have really liked it if he would have held my dad accountable for owning an illegal weapon, or at least made note of him calling an attorney before he allowed police into the house where my mother's dead body was. Again, Barney angrily wondered aloud how I got his telephone number.

"Barney, you're stupid. That's how I got it, fool!" I figured that even if I got arrested, it would be worth it. I hung up and sobbed.

I went through old e-mails my mom sent me. One of them was a voicemail message I'd saved. Her voice was beautiful and I played it over and over. All she said was, "Shelly, it's Mom. Give me a call when you get a chance." I wished I could give her a call to tell her that I was trying . . . trying to make people never forget that she should have never been treated that way. She was my mother and she deserved better than she got. To me, she had never been illegitimate. She was more than a battered woman. She was not just funny, or a joke. She was more than she knew. She was beautiful and valuable. She was amazing and endearing. She was my mom. I always believed she could have overcome her addictions. She had so much going for her. The fact that she had no money meant nothing. I wanted her to know that I was trying. I would never give up on her, ever.

I came upon another e-mail. It was dated November 20, 2008, exactly one year prior to her suicide. In that e-mail, she told me about the double suicide of her two neighbors. They had killed themselves by carbon monoxide poisoning in the garage, inside their old 1973 El Camino. My dad would later try to buy that car for my brother to rebuild, but my mom would talk him out of it, since the decomposing bodies had left an overpowering stench. It only galvanized my feelings that within the dust of the Nevada desert whirled a depressive fiber so infectious that once it landed on you—or worse—got into your lungs, it began an insidious cancer that was bound to make you want to kill yourself. I thought to myself that "Nevada" was probably Native American for "Let the white man have it. It sucks here."

As I closed those e-mails, I noticed a new one from the Care Pastor:

Michelle,

64

I have passed your e-mail onto our new lady's coordinator.

God Bless,

P.S. I hope you've notified your Bible Bunch Leader. They should be helping you on this.

Oh yes, the "Bible Bunch Leaders." Rick and I were actually the Bible Bunch Leaders of our own little bunch. The bummer? This bunch seemed to hate us and to make it even more painful, we had them to our house on a weekly basis so they could hate us right in the comfort of our own home. Well, maybe they didn't hate us exactly, but they were obviously beginning to sense that we had become "those" people, and the responses we were getting from them were mostly unbearable.

Regarding our dwindling finances, a rather opinionated woman in our group told me that I should sell my wedding ring, so that I didn't become a deadbeat. "Deadbeat," that was her word, and whenever she could make other snide comments, she would. Her inability to understand that our $76,000 a month monetary commitment would not be sufficed with my single piece of jewelry was mesmerizing. I was not, and have never been Ivana Trump or Zsa Zsa Gabor. I do not possess any amount of jewelry that would suffice our ongoing legal bills, or myriad of other business debts. Another member of the Bible Bunch informed us that she didn't need any prayers at all, for she never sinned. The phrase lingered in the stratosphere of our living room: "I never have problems, because I don't sin." The inference was obvious. People who have problems have it coming to them because they are sinful wads—that, and nothing else would be the never-ending theme to our weekly study. It was clear that we were the topic of many hushed conversations that stopped just as we entered the room: Cheshire grins all around.

Sometimes, after a Bible Bunch meeting I would ask Rick if he'd ever before seen heckling in a Bible study: Neither of us had, except for one time when a homeless man showed up in a study at church. He didn't appear to know where he was and kept asking, "Why all the talk about the Bible?" No, we had never seen sober people heckle each other in a Bible study, but make no mistake about it, we had been assigned some mockers and scoffers and regardless of how painful the sharing was for us, it appeared only mildly amusing for some members of our Bible Bunch. Sometimes they would giggle throughout our painful sharing, while other times they would just talk over us about the delicate baked pastries someone had brought or the Irish cured ham someone had bathed in sugar and butter. In actuality, giggling and talking was far better than the alternative—judgment, but that would come. Just like the subtle, dark, curled shavings over a decadent chocolate soufflé, judgment was sprinkled here and there.

In fact, it was during this time that God gave us the blessing of knowing who our friends really were. Rarely does God give you all rot with nothing to reap. Proverbs 17:17 says, "A friend loves at all times." Through that deductive reasoning, we began to easily ascertain that, even though we had overestimated some Christians, there were still others who were abundantly full of love and kindness, as though there was no end to the love they had, or could expend on others.

It was clear why my best friend, Trish, was my best friend. In my teens, I went to her house when I couldn't go home. In the toughest time of my single life she had helped me hobble through the fallout of being raped, and when my mother killed herself she was again my dearest confidante. Our neighbor, Tracey, was entirely lovely to our family. She even threw our youngest daughter, and ten of her friends, a birthday party the day before my mother's funeral. Karen and her husband—members of our wayward Bible Bunch—were God's awesome, loving servants to us, in every regard. Yes, we had Christians in our midst acting like Christians, we just needed to clear the bugs off the windshield in order to see it sometimes.

What I also learned was that sometimes there are those people, and sometimes those people are cons, and sometimes those people are genuinely hurting, but if you shut off the Holy Spirit with your own jaded, worldly-weighted discernment, you'll never know the difference. I simply know that it is a blessing to have the comfort of stable and loyal friendships that are grounded firmly in Christ, who is not moved by these worldly storms. I've also found that bad things sometimes happen to those who love God, just as he told us: "For he gives his sunlight to both the evil and the good, and he sends rain on the just and the unjust alike" (Matthew 5:45).

Chapter 5 - Traffic Court

My mother's funeral took place just days after my birthday. Three hundred fifty people gathered at a Grange Hall because my father had banned churches from the list of likely funeral venues. He also banned any religious talk, pastors, or symbols, though I secretly conspired with a close family friend who ended up giving a fire-and-brimstone sermon against the devil. My father must have been melting in his seat, but he showed no emotion whatsoever.

Songs played, a video montage glowed onto a blank screen, and my brother and I spoke. I could hardly find the words to explain my hurt and loss. I had known and denied my mother's weakness. I had seen her as the strongest person I knew and the frailest. I suspected she might end this way, but could not have stood upright everyday had I acknowledged it before it happened. Speaking at her funeral was one of the hardest things I've ever done because what I had been fighting for was over. The fight was over. My struggle against my father had ended. I no longer cared if I ever saw him again. He meant nothing. He had only been a tormentor. Circumstances had changed, but he had not. I find the only way to honor him is with honesty and my own life, not with lies and pretense. I imagine that Charles Manson has family too— probably even Christian family members. Family are just people. Some of those people are evil. If they are, let God deal with them because I have found that even in my most clever state, I'm an infant regarding them. Consider how the Bible instructs us: "I want you to be wise about what is good, and innocent about what is evil" (Romans 16:19).

All those years I had begged my mother to leave my dad, so that she could be free were gone. Maybe my parents would have both been better people apart from one another. Now, my mom was free, but where? Did she go to heaven? I would have called and demanded the reports on that every day and night, if I could have, but there was no number to call. Have I cried out to my perfect God for answers on that? I have. What did He tell me? He told me this: He is perfect and a perfect God will have the perfect answer for me when I see Him, but until then, He wants me to know that His perfect resolution for all of this is perfect because a perfect God cannot do anything imperfectly: "He is the Rock, his works are perfect, and all his ways are just. A faithful God who does no wrong" (Deuteronomy 32:4).

What I said in front of those other mourners was not that, however, because mentally I had not gotten that far. Instead, I told them of the story I had read when I was in first grade. It was Russian folklore. It was the story of how a child got lost from his mother in a neighboring village. The child could only tell the villagers that his mother was the most beautiful woman in the world. So, in order to find the child's mother, the villagers brought out all the most beautiful women to show the boy. As they paraded these beautiful women in front of the child, he protested that his mother was still more beautiful than any of the young, vibrant women. Eventually, an old, haggard peasant woman came rushing through the throng of people. She and the child met in a deep embrace. The child, with tears in his eyes, said, "See? My mother is the most beautiful woman in the world, to me." My point was that no matter what she had done to end her life, or to convolute her life with alcohol, she would always be beautiful to me.

My brother spoke about how much my mom had taught him about laughter and loving people. His speech was genuine and kind. It was the truth. Our mother had taught us as much as she could about how to see the silver lining on the biggest storm clouds. Why she hadn't been able to do that this time was confounding, except that her alcoholism had changed who she was. Also, she was limited in her scope of understanding. She had what I call a Thomas Kincaid coaster view of God. If God's word didn't fit on a Thomas Kincaid coaster, she would never have seen it. She prayed, but she prayed for herself—her wants, her needs, and her small world. It was like rubbing the Genie's lantern. If she got what she prayed for, she assumed God was pleased with her; if she didn't, she assumed God was angry with her. God is not like that. God is love, even when things go badly. He does not change because our circumstances become dire (Malachi 3:6). She could not see outside of herself. She could not see that God's ways were not her own (Proverbs 3). She could not lean on God's greater understanding in the midst of bad circumstances. In fact, I think in some way, my mom shook her clinched fist to the sky, defying God's ways and insisting that she knew better. While I believe my mother had eternal saving grace, I don't think she had the kind of grace that saves you on a day-to-day basis—the kind of grace that allows you to forgive yourself and release the things you cannot change or control to the all-powerful God of the universe.

And, because my mother had neglected to make precise delineations between all these people and my brother and me, especially since her gastric bypass when her mind seem to be in an incessant blur with the alcohol, countless people stood and gave strange and fragmented speeches, as though they had no idea she had killed herself. The cousin who had tormented my son by trying to pants him years earlier, stood for fifteen minutes and led everyone in several bizarre rounds of applause.

He began, "This woman. This woman was a success. Let's give her a hand," as though my mother was going to take the stage any minute in an evening gown or a bathing suit. "When you think of marriage, you can say 'success!'"

He could not know that my dad would be living with one of my mother's longtime friends in less than a month.

He began clapping wildly until he roused the crowd to mimic him. "When you think of kids, you can say 'success.'" I think you're a moron, I thought.

He clapped his hands over his head. "Work, success!" I would ask Doug about that.

He clapped again. "Family, success!" Are we really related? He continued clapping. I don't even know what he was saying after a while.

Then, Alex took the stage, very self-assured. As though he were trying to earn an A, he and his wife brought a couple of foam core boards with stickers and pictures glued to them. As his wife stood holding the boards, Alex droned on and on for what seemed like forever and paused gratuitously after each word, smiling at his own wit and genius. Prior to the funeral, Alex had tried to convince me that the two foam core boards would be sufficient in displaying all the family fun our entire family had ever had, but they were strangely void of any pictures of my brother, my mother's five grandchildren, or me. No, they were only of Alex, his children, his wife, and my mother. It was insulting.

Then Alex said the thing that both hurt and infuriated me the most. He pulled his wife close to his side and said, "Thank you, Keith and Michelle, for sharing your mom with us. I think we should all thank them for sharing Aunt Lena." You see, I had never chosen to "share" my mother. To me, it had always seemed more like Alex and his brood had stolen her. He had been given his own mother and when that wasn't enough, he manipulatively took mine too. To me, it was pure selfishness. In fact, what Alex and his band of merry-makers had done with my mother had always reminded me of what cowbirds do with unsuspecting host birds. Those parasitic cowbirds watch for a diligent mother bird who is about to lay her eggs, and then they lay their eggs in the same nest. Sometimes, if given the chance, they will destroy the mother bird's eggs and if they don't get that chance, they run the mother bird to death with their demanding appetites, until they grow strong enough to push her biological children out of the nest to their deaths. Alex's gratitude only confirmed the fact that he had taken my mother and stood in my way when I tried to get her clean and sober, pouring her tall glasses of brandy-colored alcohol until she no longer could determine right from wrong, good from bad. I suppose he believed it sufficient to thank me for having used her up and giving her alcoholic reprieve from my incessant attempts to get her sober. He was wrong. Being thanked for allowing others to kill my mom would never suffice as a consolation prize. It made my skin crawl.

Also, prior to the funeral Alex had hounded me about what I was going to say, telling me that he needed to approve my eulogy and video montage. He insisted on approving my eulogy for my mother. Alex is, by the way, almost ten years younger than I, and a cousin—a rude, arrogant cousin out of a lot of nice, loving cousins. I am my mother's only daughter. Who on earth did he think he was? He also told me that maybe I should have someone help write my eulogy, someone who was good at writing. Well, gee golleee Alix, mabee I do nead sum hellp cuz I jist mite pok my eye owt with a pinsil becuz Im so stooped. Was he serious? I have an English degree with an emphasis in Creative Writing. It was as though he were begging for an asphalt facial scrub—begging!

"Yeeeaaah," he said stiffly, like a teenage boy trying to figure out what Xbox game to purchase, "I would really like to get a copy of your eulogy. I'm not going to have a lot of time to go over it, sooooo—"

"Bite me," I interrupted. "Oh, I'm sorry, I'll make that more

Christian for you, since I am still a Christian. Thoust can bitest me," and I hung up on him. I was sure he had tormented countless Michelle voodoo doll look-alikes for that one. Who cared? He continued to pester me, but as is usually the case with fools, I ditched him as he became confused by a reflection of himself in a shiny metallic object.

Many of my family members were amazing. My family is not all nuts, though certainly the nuts seem to make the biggest sound when they crack. While my dad clutched his money as tightly as an old woman going to Bingo, my older male cousins and their parents—my aunt and uncle—paid entirely for my mother's funeral. As my brother and I fell apart, they beautifully and generously organized everything, including the food and the facility. Another aunt—one of the finest technical writers in all of Silicon Valley—made up my mother's funeral programs. My dad never even offered to chip in. I guess if he couldn't drag my mother's dead body out and force people to be horrified, he'd have nothing to do with it. His one attempt to contribute was his insistence that I play the song, "You Gave Me a Mountain," by Marty Robbins. The lyrics are as follows:

Born in the heat of the desert
My mother died giving me life
Despised and disliked from my father
Blamed for the loss of his wife.

You know Lord, I've been in a prison
For something that I never done
It's been one hill after another
And I've climbed them Lord one by one.

But this time, Lord, you gave me a mountain

A mountain I may never climb

It isn't a hill any longer

You gave me a mountain this time.

My woman got tired of the hardships

Tired of the grief and the strife

Tired of working for nothing

Tired of being my wife.

She took my one ray of sunshine

She took my pride and my joy.

She took my reason for living

She took my small baby boy.

And this time, you gave me a mountain

A mountain I may never climb

It isn't a hill any longer

You gave me a mountain this time

Yep, I thought the same thing. He's crazy as a goose, and frankly, that's insulting to geese. I had no intention of playing that song, ever, though there were notably some violent things I imagined doing with a record player. Rick ended up buying me a kick-boxing bag instead.

I learned that just two weeks after my mom's death, my dad sold all of my mother's possessions at a garage sale. When my mind had settled, I had asked him for my mom's first wedding ring, the paintings I had painted for her, and our family photo albums. My dad ended up selling my paintings at the garage sale—you never know when that ten bucks might come in handy. Alex and his wife took all of the photo albums—my childhood pictures—and I don't know where my mom's wedding ring went. It's fine. I was going to cut it with wire cutters and sink it in the Monterey Bay.

Though my dad toyed with me on and off, I don't know that he ever knew what to make of me. Was I friend or foe? He found me to be nothing but foe when he came to our home three days before Christmas. Tapping lightly on the front door, my dad practically sneaked into my house, not knowing that Rick was home in the back part of our house. He whispered to our kids to go to their rooms and close the doors and send me to talk to him. He was prepared to unleash his version of things. How stunned he was when Rick walked out from our office.

"Oh, Rick, you're home," he said and smiled. "Uh, yeah, I didn't realize that. You know, I just want to talk to Shelly alone—just her and me." He made it sound as though this was going to be our Opie and Andy moment.

Rick plopped down into a big chair, "Yeah, that's not going to happen."

"So, what's up?" I asked.

"Oh, not much. I sure wish you'd help me clean out the house. It's a lot of work," but my dad had already quickly quit his job and had nothing more to do than roll in piles of money, like Thurston Howl. No way was I helping him by going to his torture chamber and cleaning up God knows what.

"Yeah, well, you know I have the kids and we homeschool. I don't really have anywhere else for them to go."

He shrugged. It was a pointless argument. "Yeah, I don't know what I'm going to do. I'll tell you though, I think I know why she did it," he readjusted in the deep sofa.

I could tell that this was his purpose. This was the reason he had shown up unannounced at my door.

"Yeah, what do you think?" Because I had stayed on the Doug trail as far as it could go and I was beginning to think it wasn't Doug at all.

"Well, it was you. You were the reason she killed herself." His eyes were cold black stones as he peered at me, emotionless.

"What?" My face contorted in question mark. "What?"

Rick began to reason, "Jack, you guys were in some really serious financial problems and you know Lena was drinking . . . and on every kind of prescription med—"

"What?" I asked again. "What did you say?"

My dad looked directly at me. "It was you. She killed herself because of you."

I jumped up and screamed, "Get out! Get out of my house, you sorry piece. Get out!"

He continued to be planted to my sofa. He did not move.

I threw the plastic water bottle I was holding into a bowl of glass ornaments and they exploded, glass splintering everywhere. "Get up and get out!!! Why are you sitting there? Get out of here!" He stood and slowly made his way to the door.

"I don't care if I ever see you again." I knew I meant it even as I said it in the heat of the moment. I seldom ever say things I do not fully mean. "Don't ever call me. Don't contact me ever again." As he got next to me, I said in a calmer voice, tears rolling down my face, "Did you ever think that she might have killed herself because you beat her up for the last forty-six years, or cheated on her? Did you?"

He turned, as though he would hit me. Rick shot up from his chair, and in a commanding voice, said, "You better leave right now because you're not going to act that way in my house."

My dad glared at me for the last time I would ever see him. I slammed the door behind him. A relative told me that same month, just one month after my mom's suicide, he moved in with my mother's longtime friend, Jill. Apparently, he pressured her to quit smoking, fix her teeth, and have a face-lift, but it wasn't enough, so he moved on. My mother trusted that woman. I hope all of her dental and face work cost her a lot of money and makes her look like cat-woman.

Four months after Jill, he ended up moving in with a woman I've never met. Immediately she began sending me religious cards. I hadn't even known this woman existed until the day I received a card signed, "Love, Dad and Carla." "Who's Carla?" I asked. Relatives would fill me in. Two years went by with no response from me before she stopped sending cards. I guess her hopes of holding hands, as we skipped through a field of lilies and braided each other's hair in a giggly pillow fight, were dashed.

On the anniversary of my mom's suicide, my dad and Carla closed on their new home. They still live in hell, otherwise known as Nevada, so that's good, since they'll have to get used to the heat and sparse foliage.

Prior to kicking him out of my home, my dad had informed me that my mother's cremated remains were in a wooden box he made in seventh grade. I understood that decision to be the sole result of his penny-pinching. Sometimes, when I can't sleep, I lie awake and stare at the ceiling and wonder where that box is. In a closet? A drawer? Under his and his new girlfriend's bed? I heard that Carla won't let him keep anything of my mother's inside the house. Does that rule apply to my mother's charred remains? I cannot think too much about it because it rips at my heart like a jagged stick and it makes me cry. I wish she could have been buried near her parents and sisters, like she wanted, but just like all the deer heads my dad had stuffed and hung on the walls, he is prone to keeping the best things near to make himself look better than he is.

There are nights that anger still gets the better of me and I pray, "God, please deal with this because I don't know how." I am working on it: Always a work in progress, that's for sure. I try to think of happy puppies instead of giving people asphalt facial scrubs when anger overwhelms me.

I have to tell you the most amazing ending to our lawsuit. You will not believe it. So, a week after my mom's suicide, our poor attorney, who was working for nothing because we had long run out of money, called our adversary and told him about the suicide. He tried to appeal to his heart, but apparently our opponent did not have one, so the evil crank told our attorney to get ready for a long, drawn-out battle.

Then, a pastor friend contacted our arch nemesis and told him to let it go and try and settle it like good, godly Christians. We had already tried that, and once again, our opponent laughed at the very notion. "No way," he said. "I'll ruin those two in court."

Then, in a last ditch effort, our opponent's own pastor who had been contacted by our pastor gave a sermon on the Sunday after my mother's suicide.

He said, "There is a man here in this congregation. This man is persecuting a young, godly family who is struggling to raise their little family. I know this man knows that I'm talking to him. I'm calling you out in a public forum before God and this congregation."

A friend of mine who was in that service said our opponent did not bat an eyelash, or squirm one millimeter.

"I am calling on that man," the pastor continued, "to cease his persecution of that family. I am calling on you with the power of Jesus Christ to stop what you're doing."

That was Sunday. Monday night our evil opponent died of a massive heart attack, face down in the dirt of his multimillion-dollar estate. His wife found him hours later. He was never resuscitated, and this, my friends, is a true story! Share that one with a scoffer!

Contrary to what you might think, in our time of incessant trials, I have become enthralled by God's word. I never once doubted that He existed, though I doubted my fit into His plan. I love God more now than I did before. I am thankful for every tear I've cried that has drawn me closer to the awesome God of the universe. He and I are closer than we've ever been. When I call, He is right here: I know it. We are friends. We have been through so much together—you wouldn't believe it! When I have these mean thoughts, I go right to Him and repent because I know He took the weight of my sin on His broken body, and guess what? He forgives me every single time. I know the same God that went out to befriend a hothead like Peter, understands a hothead like me. He gets me.

In order to break away from my self-absorbed pity party, I began by reading about Stephen's stoning death. I read of the saints who were put to death and suffered enormously for no reason at all, except that they loved God, "who by faith conquered kingdoms, performed acts of righteousness, obtained promises, shut the mouths of lions," and also of others who "experienced mockings and scourgings, yes, also chains and imprisonment. They were stoned, they were sawn in two, they were tempted, they were put to death with the sword; they went about in sheepskins, in goatskins, being destitute, afflicted, ill-treated (men of whom the world was not worthy), wandering in deserts and mountains and caves and holes in the ground" (Hebrews 11:33; 11:36–38). I guess my trial wasn't so bad after all. No one ever tried sawing me in half, but I'm sure my dad and Alex dreamed about it a few hundred times.

I have come to also understand other people's reactions to our incessant tribulations because I'm certain I've responded to someone else the same way people responded to me: confused, scared, and unavailable. Being persecuted and desiring to have trouble is an unnatural compulsion. It defies everything about self-preservation, about being human; however, Scripture tells us, "through many tribulations we must enter the kingdom of God" (Acts 14:22).

Consider that even Jesus longed to avoid physically suffering. On the Mount of Olives, Jesus says, "Father, if you are willing, take this cup from me; yet not my will, but yours be done" (Luke 22:42), and then he became so troubled that "his sweat was like drops of blood falling to the ground" (Luke 22:44). No, not even our perfect Lord, Jesus Christ wanted to suffer, and yet, we are told, "now for a little while you may have had to suffer grief in all kinds of trials. These have come so that the proven genuineness of your faith—of greater worth than gold, which perishes even though refined by fire—may result in praise, glory, and honor when Jesus Christ is revealed" (1 Peter 1:6:7). Christ suffered for no other reason than to save us; we, on the other hand, suffer persecution, so that we can be more like Him in order to refine our faith.

The other thing I have learned is that when we suffer, we cannot rely too heavily on anyone other than Christ to take that burden from us. I should have never relied so heavily on the Bible Bunch, or anyone else to take away my suffering, for if they had, I would have never gained wisdom and experienced delight in the midst of my persecution. I also needed to see that the body of Christ was being the Church, but sometimes I neglected to see it, or to acknowledge it. You see, Rick and I are a private couple. We know quite a few people, but we are for the most part autonomous and private. Only in looking back could I see that all our needs were provided for. Hoards of people were not at our door with pans of casseroles or wads of money, but for two people who are fairly reserved, it was always exactly what we needed when we needed it, in the way we needed it. God will provide for you too, always in the way you need His provisions.

The other thing I learned from Jesus on the Mount of Olives, is that just when you need it most, God intervenes to give you the strength you need. As Jesus knelt and prayed to God, "an angel from heaven appeared to him and strengthened him" (Luke 22:43). When I heard that my mother had killed herself, I literally dropped to my knees and said aloud, "Elohim, Elohim, why have you forsaken me?" With the weight of this final heartbreak, I did not even imagine I would ever stand, let alone praise God, ever again. With those words out of my mouth and tears streaming down my cheeks, I felt God's hand on my right shoulder: Yes, I felt the physical presence of God reassuring me, and I heard His voice inside me say, "Be still, and know that I am God" (Psalm 46:10). And, with what happened to our legal adversary? Who, but the Lord God can do such a thing? The timing and the act were precise. It played out before our Christian and non-Christian friends equally. Everyone could see what God had done.

As far as forgiveness, I have learned to "bless those who curse you, pray for those who mistreat you" (Luke 6:28). While I will never be open to having a relationship with my dad, while he remains the same person, I do pray for him and his girlfriend. I forgive him for how he handled things, but know that we cannot have a relationship, as he is now. And, contrary to everything, I love my dad. He is part of me and I love him. Sometimes, even though he seems to have intentionally set out to hurt me, I miss him. I don't know if it's those childhood things I miss about him, and his relation to my mom, but I know that sometimes a feeling wells up in me, and I miss him and long for an opportunity to tell him how my kids are doing and have him be proud.

I do not have a relationship with Alex, either. As time passed, I felt as though he took undue pleasure in flaunting my mother's things he had taken, things that were rightfully mine. I know that I initially chose not to take any of my mother's things, but I know now that I responded that way out of my shock, horror, and deep sorrow for losing my mother to suicide. Frankly, it seemed ghastly to even think of touching her things, like vultures over a warm carcass. I can see now that Alex and his brood hastily divided up the spoils of my mother's things, taking full advantage of my lack to grasp the situation with more expedient clarity. The things I wish I'd taken are my great-grandmother's aprons that my mom wore every Thanksgiving, the photo albums my mom and I spent an entire day combing through so she could tell me who everyone was, a jade necklace my grandpa had sent my grandma when he went away to war, and the painting of big, round, purple alliums I'd painted for my mother that hung over her bed. I know it's ludicrous, but I imagine the flowers on that painting seeing my mother's soul soar away from her body heavenward—heavenward free of everything that shackled her to earth.

As for Alex, I have worked up to praying for him and his family. Sometimes I have to forgive him daily, sometimes hourly, but I forgive him because I know we had once been close. In a more carefree time, we shared our youth together. For a time, Alex had even lived with our family. I had once thought of him as a sibling. We had laughed until we were doubled over, and been close friends. I have been floored by his inability to be kind. In the middle of the night, it has awakened me on more than one night and made me cry until I had to tell God to take the pain from me, once and for all. Truthfully, I always thought that our past would win out. I believed with utmost optimism that he, too, would remember the love and fondness we shared for one another and that it would motivate him to forsake his cruel intentions and

82

meanness. It has taken years for me to realize that love and forgiveness is a choice, and so is hate and bitterness. Even though Alex is still stuck in the tar pits of his sorrow and hatred for me—hatred I hear much about through the familial grapevines—I am hopeful that he will eventually grab a stick and pull himself out because I realize that we both acted uncharacteristically. We both needed someone to blame—a scapegoat.

What I've learned from Rick, my intelligent husband, is that "hurting people are hurtful people." How true is that? I hurt Doug in the midst of my hurt, and other people hurt me in the midst of their hurt. You don't have to be great friends, but it benefits you to forgive because without forgiveness you cannot get close to God. The almighty forgiver of great offenses could not even relate to us in our stupid, unforgiving state.

As a year passed, I found God nudging me to contact poor Doug. I felt wholly and entirely stupid for having gone after that man. First of all, my mom was losing her home to foreclosure, and secondly, she was in a relationship that, by all accounts, was abusive. Some of her acquaintances were not her friends, and she suffered from depression, alcoholism, and addictions to prescription medications. Her family history alone was enough to push one over the brink. No, it was not Doug's fault. It was no one's fault. It just was. This time, I called Doug in the morning and surprisingly, he answered, although I'm sure caller ID forewarned him. At first, he was cautious. Then, we wept together and he said he appreciated my call and regretted the petty disagreements he'd had with my mother. We forgave each other because, frankly, I knew exactly how he felt.

Also, I began this book with depictions of my grandparents and I want to end with more about them because they were so central in my life. Grandpa "Wild" Bill was a storyteller. Obviously, so am I, and to forsake that would be like taping my mouth shut and strapping me to a chair in a corner. Grandma Lucy Naoma was a homemaker and deeply in love and loyal to Grandpa. I count my vocation as a homemaker the most successful thing I have ever done, and I love my husband more than anything. Grandma Lila June was a writer and an artist; I began painting in my adulthood and got a degree in Creative Writing.

And lastly, Grandpa Willard was amazing. He was the funniest person I ever met. He was rocked this way and that way by a difficult life, but he never gave up. He left behind his raucous ways—a path he seemed destined for—to pursue better. In his older years, he had his leg amputated due to diabetes. Still, his spirit was undaunted and he retained his zest for life and enthusiasm to cheer on others. His humor sustained him daily, and though he never shared his faith, he was adamant about having a particular song played at his funeral. The song was written by Kris Kristofferson and sung by Johnny Cash. It's called "Why Me Lord," and the lyrics are as follows:

Why me Lord?

What have I ever done?

To deserve even one

Of the blessings I've known

Why me Lord?

What did I ever do?

That was worth love from You

And the kindness You've shown

Lord help me, Jesus

I've wasted it

So help me Jesus
I know what I am

Now that I know
That I've needed You
So help me Jesus
My soul's in Your hand

Try me Lord
If you think there's a way
That I can repay
What I've taken from You

Maybe Lord
I could show someone else
What I've been through myself
On my way back to You

Lord help me, Jesus
I've wasted it
So help me Jesus
I know what I am

Now that I know
That I've needed You

So help me Jesus

My soul's in Your hand

Jesus, my soul's in Your hand

Crash - Bible Study

1. What generational things do you admire about your family? What generational things do you think have contributed to some family dysfunction? How can you embrace the good things about your family, while eliminating patterns of dysfunction? Read Colossians 2:8 before you answer.

2. What is the hardest thing you've ever gone through? Did you believe God was with you? Did you see Him in the midst of that terrible time? How? Looking at that time now, can you see how God used it in light of His bigger plan? What might you be missing if you can't see that?

3. Why do you think bad things sometimes happen to good people? Look at what happened to Christ and the disciples for your answer. How do the world's view of this and God's view of this differ? Read Proverbs 3 to get further understanding.

4. Have you ever defended your faith in a difficult situation? How did that go for you? Do you regret it? What would be your advice to someone defending their faith/walk to someone who opposes them?

5. When you see someone else going through difficult situations, do you automatically think, "God is punishing them," or do you think, "I bet Satan is attacking them, trying to weaken their walk. I better pray for them"? (Be honest because we've all assumed the worst at some point.) Think of a time when you had both responses to different situations. What would make you assume the worst? What would make you take a more compassionate stance?

6. If, God forbid, some of the most awful things began to happen to you in succinct procession, how would you want people to respond to you? What would you do if they responded with judgment? What would you do if they responded with compassionate kindness? How do you want to respond to others?

7. Have you, a loved one, or a friend ever been a long-sufferer? If so, what was your attitude about that? Did you remain positive, faithful, and prayerful, or did you succumb to temptation and lose faith?

8. Paul writes numerous times that he longs not to burden people with his problems. He says, "I will not be a burden to you, because what I want is not your possessions but you" (2 Corinthians 12:14). If you automatically assumed people felt this way about you when they were in crisis, how would it change your response to them?

9. Read Mark 9:28–29. The disciples wonder why they couldn't cure the demon-possessed boy, and Jesus tells them that "This kind can come out only by prayer" (9:29). How does this strengthen your idea of prayer?

10. Is there someone you need to forgive? Why won't you forgive them? Do you think holding onto unforgiveness makes life harder for them or you? Do you hope that God forgives you of all of your sins? Read Luke 6:37. Realize you will be held to the same standards of judgment and condemnation that you hold others to. How might this motivate you to forgive someone?

It's the Quiet Ones

"Because of the sinful things they say, because of the evil that is on their
lips, let them be captured by their pride, their curses, their lies."
Psalm 59:12

I do not, for the most part, enjoy camping. My first memories of
camping might have something to do with that. I was three or four
years old. We were in Los Banos, which to non-Spanish speakers,
literally means "the bathrooms." In fact, it was kind of ironic that in Los
Banos, I awoke at 4:00 a.m. to find that I needed los banos quite badly,
but there was a skunk rummaging through our campsite.

"Daaaaaddy, I have to go potteeeee," I continued to whine to my
father, as he struggled in the darkness to pull on his jeans and a t-shirt.

"Look, honey," my mother whispered as she pointed. "There's a
skunk in our campsite. We can't go out there right now."

"Aw, tell Flower to go," I grumbled. We called the skunk Flower
because of the movie Bambi and because Flower was a regular at this
campsite. Frankly, Flower is a preferable name for a skunk when you
consider the alternatives: Stinky Rodent, Smelly—the list could go on.

By the time Flower cleaned out our campsite, I no longer needed the banos. My bladder had expanded to adequate proportions, and I was asleep.

Well, as the years progressed, so did my parents' mode of camping. We went from squatters in a thin tent to deciding which television to watch, and what kind of popcorn to pop in the microwave. Now, that's my kind of camping! No more Los Banos, or Flower the unruly skunk. No, where modern conveniences went, so did we. It looked as though this camping thing just might be something I enjoyed after all! So, when a group of our church friends invited us to join them on their yearly trip to Yosemite, I was game. Heck, I'd camped in a tent before, but I asked, "Are there bears there?"

You see I am terrified, of all things, of being eaten alive. Mostly, this fear is an oceanic one. I am terrified of sharks because I am convinced that anyone as terrified of sharks as I am must give off the smell of barbeque sauce in the water. Ding, ding, ding, goes the dinner bell every time my toes hit the salty sea, and I am convinced that my pheromones mixed with intense, lesser-examined, and completely nonscientific fear-mones exude altogether the most exceptional sort of concoction a shark has ever smelled. I am certain of it! Did you know that a shark can smell blood in the water for up to one mile? Yes, if you homeschooled your children you could make them learn all the wily ways of sharks too.

Each of my children has had to do a shark study, complete with poster boards, color-printed pictures, and every conceivable scary fact attributed to sharks. As I made my daughter carve out huge jaws in her foam core board, I made her stick her head in there, just to instill in her the fear I had when my older male cousins snuck me into see Jaws, when I was just nine years old.

Still, even after all my most intimidating shark talk, those blasted kids swim way too far, making me yell from shore to their utter dismay,

"Get back in here before a shark chomps off your leg! I don't care if you're embarrassed. At least you're still in one piece . . . for now." Walking back in silence to my safe beach towel I have had to say more than once to a horrified onlooker, "Who you lookin' at?" while their little Johnny or Suzy just continue to piddle paddle around, being shark bait. Whatever. Just a note, I've also taught my kids, that in case of a shark attack, it is OK to push other children into the mouths of an attacking shark, which is a tactic I mentally devised when snorkeling in Hawaii: Something of which I'm not proud, but hey, survival of the fittest isn't just for non-Christians. All I know is that it's not easy living in California with this sort of knowledge, and it can be quite exhausting.

So, asking if there were bears was not just a simple woman's inquiry. It was more a question of whether or not I was going to die.

"Oh no. There are no bears in Yosemite—none. Especially not in Tuolumne Meadows." Something about altitude, blah, blah, blah. People actually laughed at me, though I had worked with people who had an annual camping trip to Yosemite, and one year a bear, in an attempt to get to a cooler, ripped off a camper shell door.

"Really?" I asked, and I tried to explain my secondhand knowledge of terrifying bear escapades at Yosemite, but was literally met with laughter. With all the mockery I concluded that maybe all the bear hype was just that, hype. So, we signed on and went camping in Yosemite.

One thing I noticed upon arriving at Tuolumne Meadows was that there were a lot of people with dreadlocks. Now, this isn't exceptional, since we live in California, and it's . . . well, it's California. But the ratio seemed out of whack. Then, we began setting up camp and the park ranger with his full regalia of dreadlockery came to meet us with a tag for our car and a list of items banned from the campground. The prohibition list read like an itemized statement of every single thing I had packed: No sunscreen, no lotion, no soap, no deodorant, no

94

toothpaste, no lip balm, no shampoo, which suddenly made sense of all the dreadlocks, and no conditioner. Look, it was a convenient list for the hippie sect to utilize no personal hygiene items whatsoever, and we found that running rampant throughout the park. According to the warnings posted throughout the park, this was a list of the myriad things that could and would attract a bear. Frankly, from the list, it appeared that bears had absolutely no partiality for tasty things, and I decided quickly that if a bear preferred my toothpaste and deodorant over a bag of potato chips, he deserved what he got. As for us, the whitest people on the planet, we simply could not survive without sunblock, and giving up personal hygiene, even if just for a few days would not be doable on any level.

At first, I'll admit that I was every bit skeptical at the idea that all of these items were going to attract a bear. Then, the first night—what the heck was that ruckus? Good grief! Some people arrived late into the night and were pulling their trailer in beside our group. There was a scream and some running and the sound of ripping bags and overall, the sounds of basic mayhem. As it turned out, as the people were unloading their camping equipment, a bear ran right up beside one of the men and grabbed a bag of marshmallows and took off toward the woods. Eeek! These bears were aggressive, and so much for the hippie rangers trying to convince us that bears enjoyed swigging on toothpaste and sunscreen: They were just like us—junk food junkies.

By the second night all the good stuff was put away in the bear boxes by nightfall. All that was left around the campsites was the hygienic sundries that made us non-hippies squeaky clean, snuggled tightly into our sleeping bags. Oh, and on that second night a curious thing happened. Though it was July, a usually warm time of year in California, the weather conditions dropped like a drooping dreadlock drips down the tanned back of a free spirit. It got down to 28 degrees that night. I was sure we were all going to freeze to death—that is, if the bears didn't eat us first, because you see with everything tightly boxed up in the bear boxes, the bears began coming for all of our hygiene products. Yep, just like the park rangers and all the bear signage warned, when the Twinkies, Ho-Hos, and cupcakes are all stored carefully away, bears will opt for hygiene products—hygiene products of all kinds.

That second night was a nightmare. First of all, I could not count on Rick—my better and more logical half—to take over because we had split up. There was a boy tent, which was just our son, Austin, and Rick: And there was a girl tent, our two daughters, Chloe and Sophie, and me. I knew Rick could not hear any of the ongoing mayhem because I could hear him snoring. I, on the other hand, was wide-awake. Who could sleep with the freezing temperatures? We were either going to die a Donner Party kind of death or be eaten as large human popsicles by ravenous bears. And I had to be on watch, lest someone fade away without me, um, being . . . on watch.

Much to my dismay, I heard the sounds of something large being torn away, and then shouts from the neighboring campsite. "The bear! The bear tore down the shower!" A bear had torn down a tent-like, makeshift shower stall to get to (gulp) the shampoo. Yes, they were coming at us and our shampoo! Heck, for all I knew the conditioner and the bar soap weren't safe either.

Horrified, I realized that we had just passed around our Burt's Bees lip balm. Wasn't that stuff made out of honey? Winnie the Pooh likes honey and he's quite tenacious about it. Heck, I've read tons of stories where he virtually throws all of his friends under a bus to get to honey, even little defenseless baby Roo. It was a whirlwind of mind-numbing horrors. For all I could ascertain, Winnie the Pooh was as tenacious as Jason on Friday the 13th. I had visions of a terrifying kind of Winnie the Pooh tearing through our tent for our balm-lathered lips. Our lips were coated in the stuff. The girls and I were in danger. I crawled over them and wiped their lips with the back of my pajama sleeve. Oh, my

Lord, now I was covered in lip balm—honey-coated lip balm! It's OK, I thought. I'll die a martyr's death for my children—anything for the children.

Then, another shout: "Where's the bear? Where'd it go?" I could see through the thin tent material that flashlights were canvassing the area like a strobe light. "There! There it is!" The lights flashed on our tent, our pathetic little tent.

"Aaaaagh!" I screamed. "Rick, wake up! Rick!" Snoring came back at me from his tent. "Rick!"

In a panic, I grabbed the pots and pans I had brought into our tent for just such an emergency. I began to pound them together, only to find that the new silicone-coated cookware Rick had purchased from REI was making as formidable a sound as two cotton balls clanging together—perfect silence. These hippie do-gooders were trying to rid us bourgeois squeaky-cleans from the face of the earth: First, they make up campgrounds in the middle of bear country, and then they design pots that when beaten together probably lull the bears into a virtual feeding frenzy. In an utter panic, I grabbed our younger daughter's Tinker Bell tin game box, dumped all the items from it, and began to make the most pathetic clangs one has ever heard. Maybe the bears would think us weak and too pitiable to eat, like steak laced with Mad Cow disease. I mean, if you can't even loudly defend yourself, you certainly can't be worth eating, right? It was my only hope.

By 5:00 a.m. the bear hoo-hah was over. From their night of soap-induced debauchery, they were apparently tired and went back from where they came. I too, was exhausted and freezing. The park ranger came into our camp the next morning to laugh a dull, amused laugh at the bear he called Goldy. "Uh, yeah, Goldy does stuff like that. She's funny." That was about the longest string of words we got out of that guy. Mentally, he went off the rails and just stood there gazing at nothing. I was pretty sure you had to be on something to be able to find "fun" in being terrorized all night long by bears in freezing weather conditions, and I was sure that naming your attacker does not make it any less formidable.

I continued to complain about the freezing weather and the bears, but Rick encouraged me to stick it out. I also found that his sleeping bag was rated for this kind of weather, and the kids and me—well, our bags were rated for a girl's Hello Kitty sleepover and pillow fight. In his defense, Rick's sleeping bag was the only one that would accommodate his lofty 6' 3" frame; otherwise, he would have had a pink Hello Kitty mess bunched around his knees, unable to cover the length of his body. The next night, I wrapped our middle child, Chloe, in a silver foil safety blanket I found in our car's emergency equipment. She looked like a toasty burrito. I hoped the bears had never visited a taco stand. I pulled our youngest, Sophie, into my own sleeping bag, sure that I could keep her alive with my warmth. This little trick turned out to be quite fortuitous for me because small children are like little heaters. I wrapped around Sophie like moss on the north side of a tree, but the warmth did nothing to stave off the bears. Again, they came.

This third night they seemed even more brazen. Our Tinker Bell tin was bent and busted up. I clanked it together, while I heard shouts coming from members of our own church group. The bears were in our camp!

I sniffed the air and could smell something fresh, something like the smell of coconuts. With my nose pointed toward the sky, I asked, "What's that smell?" Angel-voiced, ten-year-old Chloe perked her pretty little blond-curled head out of her foil blanket and informed me that she had put on some hand lotion she had in her purse because her delicate little peaches-and-cream hands were chapped from the cold.

"Nooooo!" I screamed. "Nooooooo, not my baby!" I tried to alarm Rick with my newfound information, knowing already it was too late from the sound of his snoring. Also, like a horror movie already in motion where you know you can't go down into the dark basement, I knew it was too late to make way to the distant bathrooms to wash it off because the bears were already on the prowl.

This, this night, would be the longest night of my life. I pulled Chloe from her sleeping bag and rubbed her hands on my pajama bottoms. I would rub off her delectable smell on myself. I would become bait for my child. As I rubbed her hands off on my legs, I patted her head and told her that I loved her. I told her, in a frantic giddiness between tears and laughter, that I had really enjoyed being her mother, and I told her run to the car and honk the horn like mad if circumstances found that I needed to shove my coconut-lathered leg into the mouth of the hungry bear. I thought that by doing so, it might make the bear choke. They must surely have a choking reflex, right? If I can choke on a chicken leg, can't they choke on my leg? With very little sleep, it sounded quite reasonable to me. Then, as one last precaution and with assurance that I would be the one the bear came for, I rubbed my lips with Burt's Bees lip balm in oozy, thick layers. Goldy, I am taking you out! Don't mess with my babies. You can have my leg and my lips, but you cannot have my babies!

I tucked Chloe back into her sleeping bag and the foil blanket. The bears were everywhere that night. There were shouts and clanging pots and pans from annoyed campers. I could hear snorting and sniffing right outside our tent, and I was sure that nothing more than just a few inches separated me from a sniffing bear's nose. It must have been smelling my coconut and honey coating, like a sugar-glazed pecan, but hopefully with that intense animal-sixth-sense, it could also smell the crazy coming from our tent, the smell that someone nutso was in that tent who was just a bear attack away from superhuman strength. I clanged the Tinker Bell tin for hours. With all the madness of someone who has been thriving on little sleep, I prayed, and out of sheer exhaustion, I finally fell over onto my sleeping bag and slept soundly.

Much to my surprise, we all actually awoke unscathed the next morning. I was not standing in the presence of God, nor was I awakened to having my lips ripped off. Overall, it was a pretty good night. We had gotten through the last and final night. It was a miracle. The Tinker Bell tin was nothing more than a twisted piece of metal origami. It had been beaten to shreds. Sophie was angry. Chloe was tired. Rick and Austin were well-rested. I was ready to go home and shower, using the most decadent-scented bathing paraphernalia known to man, leaving uncleansed hippies and bears in my camp dust. All my intense paranoia had amounted to nothing, and my anxiety had kept my imagination running a million miles a minute until I could not sustain the pace any longer.

Skip ahead five years. I was barbequing one night and felt a sharp sting on my ankle. Really, it didn't bother me too much at first, except that whatever stung me had done so within a quarter-inch of a blister I'd just gotten from some uncomfortable Easter shoes.

"Ugh," I huffed to my daughter, Chloe. "Can you believe something just bit me right there? Right on that stupid blister? Maybe those shoes are so painful they send out an attack drone while you're healing, just to say, 'Sucka, your feet are never gonna heal.'"

We laughed because my Easter shoes had been beautiful instruments of torture. I had even threatened to crawl from brunch to the car, so that Austin—my 6' 1" seventeen-year-old son—carried me piggyback to the car instead.

A day went by, and still I didn't think too much of my bug bite. Then, just like most Friday nights, Rick and I went to dinner. By the time we returned, I wasn't feeling very well. Without saying much, I quickly got ready for bed and climbed in. I told Rick that I thought I might have eaten something that disagreed with me. Within an hour, I was shaking so intensely that I was sure I had food poisoning. I was freezing. I took my temperature and found that I had a fever of 102. Yep, food poisoning, I concluded. Thirty years prior, I had gotten food poisoning, along with two hundred other wedding revelers, at my aunt's wedding. That, you might say, was the gift that kept on giving. Some of the partygoers got so ill they were hospitalized for weeks afterwards. My great aunt was hospitalized for three months!

I knew the obstinacy of terrible food poisoning and was sure that I had fallen victim, but at 2:00 a.m., while taking my temperature again, I noticed the slightest pea-sized black blister on my ankle.

"Rick," I said, teeth chattering from the intense chills of my fever, "I think I might be having an allergic reaction to something, some kind of bite." I took medicine to reduce my temperature and tried to go back to sleep.

By morning the small black blister had grown into the size of a quarter. It was a black and purple bulls-eye with a milky white outer ring. Something was terribly wrong, but I was so tired, I was not really in my right mind. Rick asked if he should take me to the hospital, but I knew the emergency room would just mean hours of waiting around. Let's face it, if you are not holding your own bloody arm for reattachment, the ER can become temporary housing. Eventually, I think most people forget why they're there and wander off down the street, either comatose or too fevered to know they should get help. I did not want to go to the emergency room.

I posted a picture of my bite on Facebook. Quickly I received two responses, letting me know that it was a Brown Recluse bite. I Googled "Brown Recluse Bite"—a definite mistake. There were pictures of mass wounds on legs, arms, fingers, necks, faces, and scalps! To compound the carnage, there were also enlarged pictures of spiders because the horror isn't complete without a villain.

Because I wanted to believe my leg would not become a mangled mass of rotting flesh, I ignored my Facebook nurse friend. "Hopefully," I told my husband, "it's a Black Widow. Black Widows are much better," and in denial of the facts, I opted to believe it was a Black Widow bite.

I called the Advice Nurse and when a doctor called back, I told him that my legs were in uncharacteristic pain, and the pain was increasingly spreading to my abdomen, kidneys, and chest. It felt as though someone had pounded me in the sides like a boxer. I could barely lie flat without pain. Pain. Pain everywhere. Pain in my arms, my neck, my face, my head, my hands, my fingers—pain everywhere, full to the brim with pain.

The doctor asked if there was a line going up my leg. Now, for people like me that is such a literal question. I envisioned wallpaper stripes going up my leg. Horrified, I examined my hurting leg. "Well," I muttered groggily, "there's a bumpy red line that goes east, and then it seems to turn north, like right there." I'm sure the doctor thought I was drunk.

"Oh," he said. "It sounds as though the infection is spreading. I'll prescribe you an antibiotic. Can someone pick that up for you?"

"Yeah, my husband can get that." I knew I was too whacked to drive and so did Rick. I started taking the antibiotic, but the bite continued to grow, as did the pain. By Monday, I had a doctor's appointment and they confirmed that it was a Brown Recluse bite. I cried because from every picture online there was no good recovery. That stupid spider had left a calling card that would mark me forever.

In my in-and-out, groggy state, I wandered aimlessly through bizarre thoughts. I was still in so much pain. I told Rick in a whisper, "Rick, I love you. I think I'm dying," and then I cried, "I feel like I'm dying. I really think I'm dying." I thought of my mom's saying: "We're always dying. It's when you stop dying, you have to worry." I hoped

I wasn't dying because I still had so much to do. I was working on this, this book. I wanted to finish it. I had no intention of trying to get published because I know I'm not famous and only famous people, or people with connections, get published, but this, this book I've been working on, it's my love letter to God. I wanted to make sure I got to finish my love letter. God had done so much for me.

I thought of Rick and the kids. God had set the foundation, but Rick had decorated the house and what a beautiful thing he had made it. Truly, Rick has given me a life that, before him, I would have only dreamt of. He loves me. He really loves me, and I love him. I really love him. He is the best man I have ever met. When I was little, I would sometimes fall asleep at night praying that God would someday give me a family that loved me and a husband that was perfect for me. God has answered those prayers tenfold. I wasn't ready to go, but maybe you're not always ready, I reasoned. I would fall asleep in and out, and I could see my grandma's sewing room, the sun beaming through her heavy curtains.

Monday I went to the doctor. They were amazed I was doing so well, although during the visit I lay over on the table and was in and out of sleep while they talked. Yes, a Brown Recluse. A dermatologist came and looked at the bite. It had grown to a 3-inch-by-2-inch oblong bulls-eye and it was oozing something disgusting. They gave me steroids and something for pain and sleep.

I stopped feeling as though I were dying. I began to feel like I was going to live. Still, my mind was a whir. Monday night it felt as though my brain had been marinating all day in something intoxicating. Rick turned the lights off in our room and I was shocked to see a myriad of blue flashing lights all around. You have to understand that we have neighbors who have motion-sensing lights on the side of their house. We have had more than one night interrupted by these sporadic illuminations. "What are they doing now?" I asked. "What on earth do they need all these blue lights for? Oh my goodness, I can't believe it."

"What are you talking about?" Rick asked.

"These," I pointed at the wall next to me. "All these blue lights."

"Honey," he paused, "there are no blue lights."

Silence.

"How about right over here?" I asked.

"No."

"Oh. OK." It took seven days for the flashing to stop when I shut my eyes.

I then decided to keep my internal mental problems to myself. This is how people get institutionalized, I thought. I also won't tell him how I've been hanging out with my grandma who's been dead for twenty years, I thought. Good grief, I was becoming more and more furious at the spider. Stupid spider. I think this is as close as I came to having "'roid rage," since they had me on steroids for the tissue damage. I wanted to kill that spider!

I thought of it. Brown Recluse. I mulled over how Jennifer Lopez got her JLo moniker. Take one letter from her first name and a couple from her last name and you have JLo. Taking the first letter from Brown and a few letters from Recluse, I figured my spider's street name: BLuse. BLuse was a jerk! I hated BLuse. BLuse had done this drive-by and tagged my ankle with his street hood crap. I seriously wanted to find BLuse and kill him! I imagined him going around my backyard barbeque with his stupid baggy pants, bragging about how he had taken out the blond giant that lived in the house. I'll get you, BLuse. You ain't no big thang. I called Terminix. Rodrigo, my favorite Terminix guy, came and doused our house in pesticides. I told him to hit the barbeque area extra hard with his poison. I wanted BLuse dead.

My venom-quenched brain began to think of ways to impress

Rick with my lucid recovery. I wanted to make sure he knew I was going to be OK and that he could soon trust me again, as his office administrator. Hmmm, think, think, think. What's a good way to show someone you've got yourself together? Then, it hit me. I always feel in control when I drive. Another time I feel in control is when I trim Chloe and Sophie's pretty long hair. That's it! I'll drive and trim their hair—at the same time! I'll have to drive on the freeway, or it won't mean anything. Anyone can piddle paddle down the street. I'll need to drive on a busy freeway. And, if I do both of those things at the same time, Rick will have to admit that my blue-light-seeing event was just an anomaly! That was a wacko fluke. Yes, I envisioned myself driving down Guadalupe Expressway toward San Jose International Airport, steering with my knees and trimming Chloe's long, curly hair. I could do it. With the right scissors, it would be easy. I mentioned it to Chloe and she looked at me like I had sprouted another head. She's fifteen. She does that a lot, but then I mentioned it to Sophie who's just ten who's usually so loving, and she gave me the same look. I decided to wait until they came around. Fortunately, as the days passed my brain detoxed and I realized they didn't even need their hair trimmed.

What I also realized was that this spider bite had been so like my creeping sin in years past, regarding my marriage. I have always loved my husband. When we met, I was startled—startled! I had never thought I would get married. I had only seen one enviable marriage in my paternal grandparents and I wasn't sure I could emulate that. If I couldn't, I had the good sense to opt out of the marriage thing, but then I met Rick. He is amazing and all those years of praying for someone perfect had paid off. He was not perfect, but he was, indeed, perfect for me.

Then, our business debacle happened. I had told Rick repeatedly not to venture into that business. I had warned and nagged, nagged and warned. The ever cautious me felt certain it wouldn't work out, and when it didn't, I was only too happy to remind him—like, a million times!

One day I remember thinking, Rick has ruined our lives. Yes, he's ruined our lives. Creditors were circling and our business opponent was suing us, and we had no money left. One day stumbled all over the next. There was no break in the stress—not one day for years. I was exhausted in my soul. Exhaustion gave way to anger, as it tends to do with me. The blessing Rick had been was becoming a memory. My love for him was waning as my anger and fear continued to grow. And, with the thought that he had ruined our lives with his decision to buy this million dollar failing business, I realized that it was a thought I should never voice. In fact, I promised myself that I would never say it to him. Later that night I surprised myself by screaming at him, "You have ruined our lives! Single-handedly you've ruined our lives!" Like a little kid with a secret too good to keep, I blurted out the thing I knew I should never say.

Rick did not fight back. Really, Rick is too strong for that sort of thing. He doesn't fight. I might punch around him like scrawny thing flitting at gnats, but he always stands tall and respectable—quiet and reserved. Yeah, it's annoying.

That's when the verse came to me, "The wise woman builds her house, but with her own hands the foolish one tears hers down" (Proverbs 14:1). I was tearing my house down with my own hands. I was the one ruining our lives. Actually, in retrospect, I think we both remained prideful for too long: He for not wanting to admit the decision was a mistake, and me for not being forgiving and supportive of him no matter what.

I was clinging to my rights and the multitude of things I deserved. I deserved an apology and restitution. In the melee of trying to appease our finances, Rick had sold my car. Of course, I constantly reminded him of that too. Simply put, I was horrid. Then, my mother killed
106

herself. From the top of my pedestal, I came crashing to the ground. I was nothing. I was a mess. I needed someone strong to shelter me, and though I had only been rotten to him, Rick reached for me and protected me, as though there had never been a cross word between us, as though I had always been his love. He treated me better than I deserved.

What I learned was that only a woman can kick her husband off his white horse, and only she can let him back on. When you feel like he's not your knight in shining armor, make sure you're letting him be the knight in shining armor. I don't think a man ever stops wanting to be viewed that way. God brought me to my knees so I would allow my husband to help me up. It worked.

In the years since then, Rick and I have never been so close. We have truly weathered a multitude of storms together. We have miscarried six times, built and lost businesses together, overcome the health issues brought on by my miscarriages, been financially decimated, and gotten through my mother's suicide. I thought we were strong before, but now we are a mighty fortress.

Before all of these things, I would have thought that our biggest threats to our marriage would have been the obvious ones—the bears and sharks, so-to-speak. In fact, in years past there was this overly flirtatious woman at church who used to literally chase Rick down, and I was sure that something like that—some unbridled hussy—would be my marriage's biggest threat. That is when I coined the term "asphalt facial scrub," and mastered the art of the death stare, but since then I have learned that it's the silent ones you have to watch for. It's the silent BLuse that bites you when you're barbequing dinner, or in other words, it's your pride. As stealthy as a prowling lion, it lurks to devour the relationships that are the most meaningful, the most significant.

There are many verses in the Bible about pride, but the one that stands out is, "Pride goes before destruction, a haughty spirit before a fall" (Proverbs 16:18). I could have held onto my pride, but I would have not been able to embrace my husband. There are things worth letting go of, so you can hold onto something worth more.

Because God richly blesses me with His lesson plan, there was more to be learned from this spider bite. One day as I was working out, God told me that He was going to stop me from working out for two weeks. For two weeks I would not be able to work out. What? There must be some mistake. Up and down, up and turn. I kept on working out, doing my step workout. I listened again and again I clearly heard that for two weeks I would be unable to work out, and just like I usually do when God tells me something I don't want to hear, I ignored Him.

Twenty-four hours later, I thought I was dying. God had stopped me in my tracks. Initially, because the pain was so intense, I didn't even remember God's warning, but eventually His words came back to me. I told Rick about it, and because my mind was not clear enough, I prayed that God would give Rick clarity so that I could know why God had done this.

Strangely, as I was praying that, Rick was at that same moment praying for clarity, even before I asked him to. God answered him. You see, we were planning to attend an upcoming family event. Some family members I hadn't seen since my mother's funeral would be there. Some of them still believed I was the reason my mother killed herself. Alex would be there. I had told Alex just months after my mother's suicide that we were done, and that if he didn't understand what that meant he should have someone else read my e-mail to him and explain the words. We were so done that I didn't want a response from him and I wouldn't read it should he happen to send one. I have not regretted putting Alex out of my life. Doing without someone who appeared to delight in my anguish is nothing I'll ever miss, but seeing him even casually would be uncomfortable.

The moment I knew about the event, I had panicked. I always feel

108

that way when I have to be around people who I believe hate me. As for working out, I always work out—almost daily, but with this looming event, I had become obsessed. It's not that my entire family is horrible, because I have a lot of family and most of my family is great, but there are some—those few—who have a propensity to judge and misjudge me, and there are also a few antagonists who have told me how much I'm hated by those few people. All the rumors and gossip have made me a nervous wreck. I have simply chosen, for the most part, to avoid family functions altogether. That way, I know for sure I can't possibly be the center of someone's hate. If I'm not around, maybe I'll just disappear. Maybe I'll become invisible. Maybe the hate will dissipate until some vague good memory of me is left in its place. I've even wondered how they can still talk about me when I've been absent so long. I never even talk or interact with anyone. Working out becomes as much my drug as Valium. It soothes my nerves and allows me to be in control—even if only for an hour or two.

What God told Rick about it was that I shouldn't be relying on myself in the first place. It was pride in myself that panicked me. Frightened of looking inadequate, saying the wrong thing, smiling the wrong smile, sitting in the wrong place, or emoting the wrong emotion had me in a dither. I knew that if someone caught my eyebrow raised at the wrong moment, or laughing too loudly or not enough, I would be critiqued about it like a prancing poodle at the Westminster Dog Show. God chose to silence me, in order to tell me that He was in control. Because I had called on Him again and again in prayer for this event, He would be there. He would have my back. He would make me more powerful through His Holy Spirit and righteousness than I could be any other way. God had stopped me from running headlong down the street in alarm, taken my face in His hands, and made me focus on Him, like a mother talking to her child. What I knew for sure was that I had absolutely nothing to worry about. No gift I could give, or dress I could wear, no words I could say would make this event anything God did not want. He, and He alone, was in control.

That event ended up going exceedingly well. It was a blessing in every way. I was able to reconnect with family I hadn't seen in years. I enjoyed the beauty of the moment, which was a God-glorifying event. On the way to the event, our little band of five prayed in the car. I felt the Holy Spirit overwhelm me. I knew that no matter what happened my God was still God of the universe, and I would still be driving home with the four people I love the most. God used BLuse to allow me to be loose, so that I would not focus on sinful, faulty me; instead, I could focus on wonderful, awesome Him.

It's the Quiet Ones—Bible Study

1. Is there a relationship that is broken in your life? Why? Do you think that pride keeps you from reconciling with this person? If you were to discuss it with God, what do you think He would want you to do? Pray about it now, talking to God as you would a friend.

2. Is it more important for you to be right, or right with God? Consider these verses: "Do all that you can to live in peace with everyone" (Romans 12:18), and "And let the peace that comes from Christ rule in your hearts. For as members of one body you are called to live in peace" (Colossians 3:15). When is the last time you chose to be right before God, rather than right in a dispute?

3. What things are you prideful about (appearance, materialistic possessions, career, family, children, education)? How does your pride about that affect your ability to get close to others? How does it affect your ability to get closer to God?

4. To you, what is pride?

5. To God, what is pride? Consider the Pharisees. Also, read Psalm 101:5 and Proverbs 8:13. What other verses do you know about pride?

6. In Psalm 105:36, it says that God "killed the oldest son in each Egyptian home, the pride and joy of each family." Why do you think God killed "the pride and joy of each family"? Has God ever "killed" your source of pride? If so, how did it change your perspective and attitude?

7. Why does God want us to be humble?

8. Can God be God when you are pridefully on the throne? Do you see any adjustments that need to be made in order to make sure God is where He needs to be in your life? If you don't see God working in your life through blessings, miracles, and His presence, be sure you are not standing in the way.

The Swinger Set

"The acts of the flesh are obvious: sexual immorality, impurity and
debauchery."
Galatians 5:19

I'll assume if you don't live in California, you cannot even
comprehend such a predicament, but our neighbors were people who
remodeled their entire backyard to accommodate every swinger within
a hundred-mile radius. In case you don't know what a swinger is, it is,
according to Wikipedia, "non-monogamous behavior, in which singles
or partners in a committed relationship engage in sexual activities with
others as a recreational or social activity." In my opinion, it's pure gross-
osity, which is a word I could not find on Wikipedia.

Instead of putting in a pool to entertain friends, or a fire-pit to relax
with a glass of merlot after a long day, they made Swinger Haven: a
petri dish for every venereal disease known to man, and some yet to be
discovered. The very thought makes me shiver and want to go suck my
thumb in a corner, curled up in the fetal position.

I had been suspicious for some time. You see, I had tried

befriending these people over the course of a few years with my cookie delivery tactic. I have found that you can talk to virtually anyone while carrying a warm plate of homemade cookies. So, when we moved into what we devoutly believed was a home provided to us directly from the hands of God, I was not going to be lazy about my mission work. I was like clockwork with my cookies. On a cold, blustery day, what better thing to have than a plate of warm cookies? On a sunshiny day, what better thing to enjoy than a plate of warm cookies? On Easter? Warm cookies. Christmas? First day of Spring? Groundhog's Day? The White Sale at Macys? Warm cookies.

Look, warm cookies might seem trite, but it got my foot in the door with the most elusive people on our block. Up until then, even though they had lived in that house for well over twenty years, no one knew them, their names, or anything about them.

What I found was that they had met while trying to become upwardly mobile in a cult, and they had managed to raise one daughter. She had ended up being a stripper they never saw, but while living in their home, she had been on the brink of death at least five times from starving herself. The other thing I found was that they were self-proclaimed Jews, which made me hopeful, for if they believed in the same God of the Bible, we at least shared that basic foundational principle.

Well, then came the talk of how they were going to remodel their home. With shared ideas and talk of that, since we'd just remodeled our own home, Rick suggested that I help them with interior design ideas as I was taking interior design classes at a local college. I did, but it was on my first consultation visit that I realized something was glaringly amiss. You see, even though they had numerous social gatherings with hoards of people on multiple occasions, they had absolutely no furniture— none! Instantly, I wondered where all of those people sat. How did they eat their food? Where did they put their drink glasses?

As I talked with the woman for an hour or so, I asked, "Where do you sit when friends come to visit?"

She responded, "Weeeell . . . we mostly stretch on the floor. Yes, we do a lot of stretching when our friends come over. Everyone's into yoga and stretching is so good for you." Her eyes glazed over and she stared, smiling a big, broad grin at me. She seemed eternally happy.

Stretching? With friends? On the floor?' My mind was a whirl of what that must look like. Weird, I thought, but I said, "Oh, OK. Well, I'll try and come up with something."

She caught me as I began to leave and said, "And, you know, if you could come up with something that could hang down maybe just two feet off the floor . . . lanterns or mobiles, maybe even wind chimes." She put her hand down low to show me the height she had in mind. "Because we're all down low . . . on the floor, stretching."

Just then a light bulb went off in my head. They were not stretching! I nearly gasped. Two feet off the floor meant you were lying on the floor—I stretch before and after I run and I know that some of the best hamstring stretches are done pretty much while you're still standing. Stretching indeed! I was horrified. I could not get out of that house fast enough.

Being a professional, however, I put together some sketches, and after a few weeks of prayer I had the courage to go present them to her. I was pretty pleased with myself for coming up with ideas that involved no furniture. It was a taxing assignment, but I did it!

It was in this meeting I was relieved to hear her say, "This is the year that I'm going to give up my preconceived ideas of religion and spirituality and just give everything a try." That was music to my ears. I let her continue. "Yes, Michelle, I am just going to try everything, embrace it all." She put her arms out and swooped them back in to her chest, as though grasping a big load of air.

116

"Wow, Leah, I am so glad to hear you say that. I've been praying for you and I was hoping you might join me for a church service. You know, Christ gives me so much peace, and I think Christ can give you peace too."

Her mouth was suddenly agape. "What? I can't do that, I'm Jewish!"

"Oh, I understand, but you just said you were going to give everything a try," I gently prodded.

"Not that!" She laughed. "You know, just spiritual things."

Actually, I did not know, but I soon found out what "spiritual things" she had in mind. As weeks passed, she and her husband put in a saltwater pool. Only the large pool portion was heated to accommodate perfect body temperature, and the dunking pool was a two-person pool meant for cool downs. There was also the sauna area with a bed, an erotic picture, and an unusual swing that I told our children they could not sit in when Leah and her husband, Phil, insisted on giving us a tour.

Still, we had no solid proof of what they were doing, only an inkling of an idea that things were not copasetic. In fact, Leah and Phil told us to be prepared for anticipated groups of people who would be borrowing the healing benefits of their pool for aqua-therapy sessions.

That is when it began. One Saturday afternoon an exotic car pulled up in front of their home. Like wings, the doors to the car smoothly glided open, and two people got out. Now, I have only seen pictures on television, but I called to Rick over my shoulder, "Either they are having a pimp and ho party, or a pimp and ho have just arrived at their home for some aqua-therapy." Rick and I leaned toward our plantation shutters while the two visitors walked right into Leah and Phil's house. They left nearly six hours later.

After that, the people came in far greater numbers. When new neighbors, Rob and Vicky, moved into the newly built two-story house directly next door to Leah and Phil, I asked Rick if I should warn them, but he said no, since we really didn't have concrete evidence of what was going on.

Well, the morning after their first night, Rob marched across the street in shocked dismay. "Dude," he huffed, "you don't even know what's going on over there! It's . . . it's . . . it's obscene!"

"See Rick!" I turned to Rick. "I knew it! Stretching, yeah, everyone has their friends over to stretch all night long. How normal is that?" I exclaimed.

Rob continued, "I don't even know how I can let the kids upstairs ever again. Vicky's on the phone with her mom freaking out." He looked backwards over his shoulder at Leah and Phil's, and shook his head. "I can't believe people would do those things outside, in front of other people. We planned on getting a climbing structure for the kids on that side of the yard. We can't do that now. One big swing up in the air and they'll see things that . . ." He couldn't continue. His words faded off as he seemed to struggle with the reality that he had just moved his sweet young family next door to a hedonist haven.

After having our fears confirmed, we began a silent battle. I would boldly glare at people rumbling down the street to stop in a screech in front of my home, only to run to Leah and Phil's home with their cars parked askew. It was obvious that these people were in a frenzy to get to Leah and Phil's. They sped crazily up and down the street, sometimes backing up a hundred feet, until they finally ascertained their final destination. When they did, they would park up on curbs, out in the street, and blocking driveways. It was as though Leah and Phil had announced a garage sale on money. It was horrible.

With some research and questioning, we found out that most of the swingers were local, though sometimes a traveler would come from far away to get to Leah and Phil's. We knew this because one night around eleven o'clock, Rick watched a guy lurking around the neighborhood. Rick ended up questioning him, but the wayward wanderer said he didn't exactly know the names of the people he was visiting, just that he had flown in from another state and was there for the night. With greater research, we learned that there are random networks of perverts looking for exactly this type of thing. They get an address, a telephone number, and an invitation to wallow in absolute debauchery.

Thank goodness for my 6' 3" husband who, though especially kind, can pose an intimidating figure when needed, since he was able to run off the aforementioned pervy swinger with just a few abrupt words. I, on the other hand, am not as intimidating in stature, even though I am certain that I am quadruply crazier than anything Rick could even imagine. One time, I strolled down the street to find a slovenly, obese man, chomping on cake, leaning his big plump arm on the top of his car, and staring at my sweet son like a hawk stares at an unblemished white bunny. Unalarmed, my son just continued to carve lines in our grass with the lawnmower, while the man continued to ogle.

I stopped abruptly, with the car separating us. "Can I help you?" The rotund man shoved the last crumbs of the cake into his mouth with a fat finger. "'Cause let me tell you this, you filthy pervert—I live here, and if you know what's good for you, you'll get your big, fat tail in your car and get out of here!" I am mother, hear me roar!

The man's eyes shot open wide as he dove into his noisy jalopy and quickly took off down the road.

There were many days just like that when I felt that the Holy Spirit was trying to lasso me, keeping me out of prison and off crime blotters. But one day—one day in particular proved too much. We were barbequing at Rob and Vicky's house. With his lofty height, Rick got an unfortunate peek at a stout, naked man in the buffet line at the swinger house. Then our daughter, Chloe, only eleven at the time, saw a naked man while riding her bike down the street. I felt certain that God was

119

saying I had permission to hurt people, but couldn't find it anywhere in the Bible. You can do a word search on Bible Gateway and you cannot, regardless of how hard you try, find the word "pulverize" anywhere!

Then, as Rick ran home to get some barbeque sauce, he realized that someone from Leah and Phil's had run into his car and crunched his bumper. Already that day there had been three shifts of swingers. The first shift had come at 8:30 a.m. The second shift barely missed the first and arrived at 12:30 p.m. Then, the last and most tawdry shift had arrived around 5:00 p.m., which meant they might stay all night. The last shifts were usually those prone to drink alcohol and were not as peace loving and earthy as the others.

Rick had to go apprehend the swinger in question and figure out why a driver had plowed into his bumper, leaving a perfect indentation of their car's license plate. Fortunately, as he peered over the fence to call to the owner of the burgundy minivan, the woman was still clothed. I felt as though it was God's good mercies to allow such a thing. Well, the woman came across the street and strangely denied doing it, though her license plate frame had left a perfect embedded mark on Rick's bumper. Then, as though orchestrated by God in heaven, as though in slow motion like a scene in a movie where you cannot believe what you're about to hear, the woman said, "I did not hit your car, and I wouldn't lie about it because I'm (slow motion time) a C-h-r-i-s-t-i-a-n."

Oh no, she didn't! My hand shot into the air as though I was doing an exorcism in some Cajun witch doctor hut. "In the name of Jesus Almighty, get behind me, Satan!" Rick's face dropped. Hadn't he told me to go in the house? Well, this mightily disobedient wife stood firmly on the lawn, calling up verses and flinging them at her like boomerangs.

When Rick finally shushed me, the woman began, "Look, you're a reflection of me and I'm reflecting love back onto you, while we reflect onto each other in our one united reflection of love."

120

Rick and I looked at each other, bewildered. The woman stopped and smiled a big, glassy-eyed grin I'd seen a million times from Leah and Phil.

"Say what?" I turned to Rick. "I think they had the heat turned up too high on their swinger sauna." This woman was rambling the craziest stuff I ever heard, and I'm from California—I've heard my share of crazy ramblings!

Pretty soon Leah and Phil came marching across the street to defend their "friend," though the woman had already admitted she had never met them before. I told them everyone in the neighborhood had come to the revelation that they were not doing aqua-therapy, as they had claimed. All said, there were heated words exchanged back and forth. Nothing too ridiculous, except that they said we were unrealistically paranoid about the risk their so-called friends posed to our children. To compound the idiocy of it, they insisted that their daughter was not harmed by the exposure to such things. I felt as though it would be too hurtful to point out the obvious, since reality spoke well enough for itself. Saying too much would have been, in my opinion, cruel.

At this point, years have gone by. Leah and Phil are still having their parties. Their "friends" park farther away, so as not to disturb the neighbors. In fact, we found their website and they specifically warn patrons to never park in front of our house. That might be the result of me telling them they are free to do what they want, and I am protected by free speech to yell, "Pervert," or "Freak" at people. Who knows, maybe I have sporadic turrets? I think Rick would be my best witness.

"Yep," I said, "thank goodness for our American freedoms because I might even get lawn placards welcoming all your freaky friends into the neighborhood. Why should you have all the freedom?" I taunted.

We've also found that their parties are oftentimes called "Snuggle

Parties," and can go on all night long. You would not believe the people that participate. My main question: Why do all the people who should be covered by at least three or four layers want to be naked?

They are no longer friendly because we have called out what they wanted to remain hidden. At first, I regretted having dissolved our cordial acquaintance, since I felt we had come so far. It took me a while to see it for what it is: Leah and Phil are as impassioned about their lifestyle as I am about bringing nonbelievers to Christ. If you doubt their commitment then you need to understand the time, energy, and expense they afforded to make their backyard into a den of depravity. They overlooked no expense in their pursuits, and although I pray for a different outcome, we may always be at an impasse.

If I have learned anything, I have learned that as Christians, we should be as impassioned to spread the Gospel of Jesus Christ, as Leah and Phil are to spread their ideas of groovy love. Recently I completed a Bible study with a group of women. One of the women in the group said that her favorite female Bible character was Jezebel. Now, at first that seems shocking and incongruent to a Christian, Bible-believing woman; however, when you understand her explanation, you can better appreciate her reasoning. First of all, Jezebel was determined: She never lost focus. She was committed to her god, as we should be committed to ours. Consider this verse: "There was never anyone like Ahab who sold himself to do evil in the eyes of the Lord, urged on by Jezebel his wife" (1 Kings 21:25). Now, consider how a Christian wife with that same zeal, urging her husband on toward godly servitude that promotes the will of God and the goodness of His divine character could be eternally advantageous: wow, the things that could get accomplished!

Another thing I came to realize is that even though these particular circumstances seem crazily out of the realm of Christ-like things, they are exactly the same sort of problems Jesus dealt with in his day. In fact, they have been dealt with all throughout the Bible. In the Old

Testament, there were shrine prostitutes that presented their sexual activities to their gods. In the New Testament, Jesus speaks directly about sexual immorality when he says, "Anyone who looks at a woman lustfully has already committed adultery with her in his heart" (Matthew 5:28). And, Jesus addresses the nature of the issue when he says, "For it is from within, out of a person's heart, that evil thoughts come—sexual immorality, theft, murder, adultery, greed, malice, deceit, lewdness, envy, slander, arrogance, and folly" (Mark 7:21–22).

What I appreciate about Jesus' summation of this is that there is no difference between sexual immorality and something much more acceptable in society, like arrogance. They are all evil results of a darkened heart. Knowing this has allowed me to continue to pray for my neighbors, to have mercy on them, and to never give up hope that at some juncture there might still be a chance to introduce them to Jesus. I know that I cannot be yoked up with them in a deep, intimate friendship, claiming to condone their choices, "For what do righteousness and wickedness have in common? Or what fellowship can light have with darkness?" (2 Corinthians 6:14), but I am convinced that these neighbors pose no greater threat than missionaries face in the mission fields all over the globe.

In fact, it has been a struggle to keep in mind that though their deeds draw out of me a visceral response, it is no more appalling to God than my telling a lie, or using profanity. Consider what Paul wrote to the Corinthians:

I wrote to you in my letter not to associate with sexually immoral people—not at all meaning the people of this world who are immoral, or the greedy and swindlers, or idolaters. In that case you would have to leave this world. But now I am writing to you that you must not associate with anyone who claims to be a brother or sister but is sexually immoral or greedy, an idolater or slanderer, a drunkard or swindler. Do not even eat with such people. What business is it of mine to judge those outside the church? Are you not to judge those inside? God will judge those outside. Expel the wicked person from among you (1 Corinthians 5:9–11).

It's easy to understand that by judging those inside the church, we do so in order to keep the bride clean and pure for her bridegroom, who is Christ, but when we judge those outside the church, we hold the world to an unrealistic standard it can't possibly attain without the cleansing blood of Christ. No, you cannot judge nonbelievers the same way you judge believers.

Whatever I might think of my neighbor's activities, they are as lost as any tribesman who has never heard the name of Christ. Even though I might righteously respond to a woman in their midst claiming to be a Christian, or distance myself from their seemingly unsafe and perverse undertakings, I cannot hold them to an unrealistic, Christ-like standard. Instead, I can pray for them to experience the saving grace of Jesus Christ, for as it is written, "Whenever anyone turns to the Lord, the veil is taken away," and "Where the Spirit of the Lord is, there is freedom (2 Corinthians 3:16–17).

The Swinger Set - Bible Study

1. What sins do you have a difficult time dealing with in others? How might Satan use these types of sins to keep you from sharing the love of Christ?

2. Considering your answer to question number one, what does the Bible say about such sins? How is this particular sin viewed in God's eyes? How can God's view help you change your view of that sin?

3. In Luke 4:18, Jesus recounts, "The Spirit of the Lord is on me, because he has anointed me to proclaim good news to the poor. He has sent me to proclaim freedom for the prisoners and recovery of sight for the blind, to see the oppressed free, to proclaim the year of the Lord's favor." Even though Jesus says he brings freedom to the oppressed, why do most living outside the church believe that Christianity is the ultimate bondage? How can we help unsaved people to see that sin, not allegiance to Christ, is the ultimate bondage?

4. So that we are not enablers of sinful behavior, what can we do to reveal Christ to a nonbeliever embroiled in a sinful way of life that represents a sin we find personally repulsive or offensive?

5. Should we hold non-Christians to Christian standards? How is this unfair? When I'm compelled to do this, I think of someone forcing me to walk a tightrope across the Grand Canyon, which is particularly frightening with my fear of heights. How is having Christian expectations of non-Christians similar?

6. Read John 12:47. If Jesus says he did not come to judge, should we judge others? Why is Christianity oftentimes so fraught with judgment?

Surprise! You're Going to Fail!

"The Lord is the one who goes ahead of you; He will be with you. He will not fail you or forsake you."
Deuteronomy 31:8

On my seventeenth birthday, my parents decided to give me a surprise party. The real surprise was that I was working at a pizza parlor, and my mother had invited my entire family and several of her coworkers to come to my work, order several pizzas, a dozen pitchers of beer and soda, and take over the banquet room for an overwhelming birthday surprise. With well over thirty messy partygoers descending upon my workplace, I can aptly say that nothing has ever surprised me more.

First of all, the crush on the kitchen was more than we had anticipated. It was frankly a bit exhausting. After closing, I had to stay later than normal to clean up the aftermath of my party. The excess of dirtied pizza pans, plates, silverware, and drink glasses had piled up the kitchen sink. We seldom got crowds in the banquet room, especially groups that stayed late. Shoving crumpled tissue paper and bent boxes into a large garbage bag, I thought, Wow, did my mom think this out? Because this is just about the worst birthday party ever!

When I got home, the street was lined with cars. To me, the party had morphed from surprising to full-on shock and awe. This was exactly the type of party that no one wants to have the night before their scheduled SAT test, and yet, that is exactly what I was looking at. Weeks in advance, I had scheduled to take the SAT the very day after my birthday. (The SAT is a globally recognized college admission test.) I had told my mother numerous times about it, shown her the postcard reminders, and conveyed on more than one occasion my intense fear of taking the test. As I surveyed the street, I could see that my mother had not adequately understood the significance of the SAT.

Though it was normal for my parents to have parties on most weekends, a party on this scale seemed out of whack, even for them. Though I knew very little about the SAT—being the first one in my family to consider college—I surmised that this type of debauchery could not be conducive to proper test preparation.

Once inside our house, I realized that the number of people who had been at the pizza parlor had more than doubled. There were well over seventy people inside our home and mulling around poolside. I briefly walked by the kitchen and hesitated to focus on the meadow motif clock that hung on the far wall. In the inner circle of sweet resin ladybugs, faux wood, and daisies, two metal hands confirmed that it was already 11:37 p.m., and this party was just beginning. My heart sank.

It started to dawn on me, like that realization you have as you first smell burnt cookies and you know they're too far gone to salvage, this surprise party for me seemed a ruse, a farce, a smokescreen for something else: Wandering through smoke-filled rooms, people seemed to barely notice that the party girl, the guest of honor was even home. It sure didn't seem like a birthday party for me. Then, it hit me!

129

My uncle, my parents' dearest partying companion, was turning forty this year. Through a billowy cloud of cigarette smoke I saw him, my uncle, leaning on one of his drinking buddies. Really? What was one of my uncle's drinking buddies doing at my seventeenth birthday party? Clearly, my mother had put up the detour sign to distract me. Heck, she had wallowed in mud to throw me off the scent, but I was home and I was on to her! Clever as a fox, she had handed me a last-minute surprise party for a couple of reasons: First, it delayed my arrival, and she had probably had her fill of hearing about that blasted SAT test, whatever that was. Secondly, she couldn't in good conscience give my uncle a big, raging party without giving me something, even if it was door #2, the consolation prize of a free, broken-down donkey named Bo-Bo.

I went upstairs to de-pizza myself. The smell of pizza dough, pepperoni, and garlicky sauce was under my fingernails and in my nostrils. Trying to open the door of the bathroom, I found it locked. I had to wait an inordinately long time and finally knocked. Quickly, a strange woman exited, shuffling past me, seemingly without any knowledge that I lived there and that it was my bathroom she had just been in.

I went in and locked the door behind me. Suspiciously, I looked around and sniffed the air. "Oh no. Imagine she did not just puke in here," I told myself. No, no, I don't smell anything funny. It's pizza sauce and cigarettes, that's all, I tried to convince myself. Maybe it's just weird perfume. I laughed a little catching my ashen, twisted face in the mirror. Yeah, perfume that smells an awful lot like puke!

I began wiping off mascara, and cleaning my face. There was a jiggle of the doorknob. "Someone's in here," I said over my shoulder, toward the door. The door jiggled more feverishly, and then excited tapping. "Go away! I'm in here and I live here! The tapping stopped abruptly and I heard slow, disheartened footsteps head down the hallway. With a heavy breath, I sighed. "It's OK. If I go to sleep quickly, I still have six hours to sleep. That is . . . if I fall asleep in six minutes." I laughed to myself, a miserable knowing laugh. "Well, six hours is almost eight hours—just a couple hours off."

I climbed into bed and pulled the blankets up around my neck. I lay staring at my ceiling, but all I could focus on was the pounding bass from the music wafting up the staircase. It was the agitated heartbeat of our home, induced into possession by the voodoo dancing of inebriated natives. For many sleepless hours I stayed in my room, on my bed, in total submission, knowing that to fight was futile. I looked at the red numbers glowing from my nightstand alarm clock. It was 2:43 a.m. Inhaling deeply, I could still smell Italian spices, mozzarella cheese, and pizza sauce on my skin and up my nose. That smell was in my pores.

Just then, I heard pounding down the hallway at the bathroom door. A man's voice slurred, "Kelleeee, come out. Come out of there!" He kept pounding on the door. I went to my bedroom door, and peeked out to find a friend of my uncle leaning on the door with one arm, clenching a copper-colored beer bottle in the other hand. He was staring at the locked door as though he expected it to talk back any minute.

"Hey! Hey, Kenny!" I snapped. "Can you be quiet? I've got to be up for the SAT in just three hours." He looked at me, annoyed, and I narrowed my eyes at him. "Yeah, Kenny . . . well, you need to keep it down, 'cause I'm Lena and Jack's daughter and I live here!" I slammed the door behind me. What was I thinking to mention the SAT? And, for crying out loud, telling him I was Lena and Jack's daughter didn't carry any weight. He probably didn't even know who they were, though he was prancing around our house like he owned it. I'm sure everything I had just said to him was as foreign to him as if I'd told him I was taking off for Mars in the morning. He couldn't care less because he was drunk as a skunk.

Clearly upset by his partner's unhurried pace, he pounded again. "C'mon, Kelly, right now!" Just then, I opened my door again to unload another round of demands, but instead another woman met him at the door. Knowing him, she moseyed between him and the door.

"Sheeeee's not in there," she snarled. Clearly, she was drunk too. They were all drunk, weaving and swaying back and forth. It was like watching fish float around in the murky waters of a dirty fish bowl.

"Where is she?" he said as he fell back into the wall. He was belligerent and testy.

"Well, Kenny," the woman said in her best hissy kitty-cat voice, "She's sick of you following her around and hanging all over her, slobbering all over her every time she sits down." She glanced at the locked door with a sideways smile. "For your information, Kelly and I locked that door with no one inside it . . ."

Great! I thought. I'll have to pick the lock on my own freaking bathroom now. I will NEVER get to the SAT!

" . . . to make you think," she continued, "that she was in there, so you'd leave her alone for a while."

"Wheeeeere is sheeeee?" Kenny hissed.

"I'm not telling you, sooooo you just leave me alone." The woman turned on her heels, as best she could, and attempted to walk away.

Awkwardly, Kenny's hand fumbled to grab the woman's arm. "No," he said, "I will not. You tell me where Kelly is, right now!" They both staggered to opposing sides of the hallway.

"I'm telling you, Kenny, if you don't leave me alone, I'm gonna punch you right in the face." Oh c'mon! No way, I thought.

"C'mon, you guys, just go back downstairs. You shouldn't even be up here, and I have the SAT . . ." I stopped short. Even I was getting sick of hearing about the SAT.

"Oh yeah? You are going to punch me? Well, I dare you! Go ahead and punch me!" And with those words barely out of his mouth, the woman drew back her fist and punched Kenny in the face. Stiffly, as if in slow motion, his head jerked backward. Like a flimsy bobble-head on the dashboard of a car, his vacillating head eventually swayed to a stop, as he tried to account for what had just happened.

"Ah, c'mon. No way!" I said.

Regaining his composure, as though experiencing the turgor pressure of a watered flower, he said again, "Yeah, well I dare you to do that again!" And, with that, the woman drew back her fist once more, aimed through squinted eyes, and released another blow to Kenny's face.

I shut my door, leaving them to their smack fest in the hallway. No way was I going to do anything well on the SAT, unless they had a section on my recent observation of fighting drunkards. The test was in just a matter of hours and I had been awake nearly twenty-four hours. Had I complained to anyone at my party I would have been ratted out as the uptight, goody-two-shoes girl who thought she was too good to party with everyone. And, in some bizarre Tour de Crazy, it would have been quickly assessed that I was obviously profoundly stupid. I mean, who else has to study all the time? Who else has to read all those books? Who else in our family had ever had to take the durned SAT anyway?

From what I heard, Kenny dared that woman to hit him in the face one more time. She punched him a total of three times in the face. After that, he dropped to the floor outside my room and bawled like a drunken baby. The only thing more annoying than two drunks fighting is one drunk crying loudly. There was no filter on his volume, so he just sputtered and blathered on and on. The minutes multiplied into an hour.

Finally, because he had not passed out as I hoped he would,

I peeked out my door one last and final time. "Look," I hissed venomously, "I understand that woman hit you." He looked down toward the floor through his upright knees and let out a sob. "Yeah, I know, Kenny, but if you don't shut up—I mean, shut up for good—I'm going to hit you again!" He looked bewilderingly up at me from his slumped position on the floor. His head bobbed as though he were dodging imaginary gnats. "Just shut up! No one wants to hear you cry, so shut up!"

I slammed the door behind me, and fell back hard onto my bed. It was over. It was almost 3:23 a.m., and it was over. Even if I fell asleep now, I might never wake up, so I consoled myself and knew that it was over. The party beast had won—the academic bird had been squashed by a keg in my backyard. It was over.

When I got up, the house was still discharging steam from just being released from the bowels of the drunken beast. Everyone slept silently. My joints ached from no sleep. My hair and skin still smelled of pizza sauce and cigarette smoke. Kenny and Kelly were gone. For a quick breakfast, I grabbed a few stale chips from a bowl on the kitchen table as I headed toward the door. I shut the door gently behind me, got into my Chevette, and headed toward a foreign part of town to take a test I would assuredly do poorly on.

When I arrived at the test site, an uppity high school in an exclusive area, I felt like a street urchin peeking in a window at all the normal people. Girls were well dressed with freshly shined faces and crisp white headbands, like they'd just gotten out of parochial school. My hair was pulled back in a wretched ponytail, stray hairs flitting around like Medusa snakes, and my face showed droopy signs of sleeplessness. Ugh, I thought. I put on my best "I-don't-care-about-you" face, sat nonchalantly in a stiff metal chair and journeyed forth with sharpened #2 pencil and empty bubble scantron.

Months later when I got my results, I knew they would hinder,

134

rather than help me get into a good college. I never signed up for the SAT again. I was afraid that something even more catastrophic would hinder me from doing well. Maybe I'd be given another surprise party and we'd all mud wrestle each other until 4 a.m. In any case, I knew that getting into college for me would not be a slam-dunk.

I was right. Those SAT scores lowered my chances to go directly to a four-year college. Instead, while all my friends went to four-year colleges, I went to a community college, and then transferred to a four-year college to finish my degree. I learned that sometimes when you are sure it's over, that you cannot possibly get ahead no matter how you try, God might just be redirecting your path a bit. You'll get there—you'll just get there in God's timing, in God's way. If I had known God at the time, I might have been comforted by these truths, but clearly I was not from a Christ-centered home.

More than once throughout life I've been reminded that life is not as easy as I'd prefer it. It seemed to take forever to meet my wonderful husband, though in reality I was only twenty-six when we married. I miscarried a total of six times, and I have struggled miserably to emotionally connect with my birth family until God blessed me anew with a family all my own. From where I have stood, there are people who seem to have all the cards stacked in their favor, but for the most part we all carry a burden that does not allow us easy, unhindered, unobstructed favor.

Initially, I did not get into a four-year college. Based on my SAT scores, I couldn't have been accepted at a four-year college right out of high school. Instead, I went to a junior college, worked several odd jobs, and struggled through an overly oppressive and abusive relationship. Looking at it that way, it seems like life was dismal and bleak, but God's plan for me was anything but.

Those numerous and diverse odd jobs gave me invaluable experiences. I met people and did things other people my age would have to wait years to experience. The relationship I had with an abusive and oppressive person allowed me to get that sort of emotional mischief and drama out of my system, so that I would realize being alone was better than being harmed, and that waiting for a mature, godly man was best of all. Going to a junior college saved my family money and, in turn, my parents offered to fully pay for my last two final years of college wherever I gained acceptance.

It's not what I planned, but it's exactly what God had in store. Sometimes, what we think we were meant to have derails us completely. I have a friend who is fixated on living in a particular wealthy area in Silicon Valley. He cannot retract from the idea or notion that his life would be better if he and his family lived in this wealthy area. He talks of it incessantly, until all he thinks about is what he doesn't have. Had I continued to focus all my energy on my initial plan, I would have become too discouraged to attempt something else and I might have driven away new friendships and opportunities.

For me, taking the SAT was just a stepping-stone to the bigger picture. It took me years to see that the debacle of taking that test was probably a blessing in disguise. Scoring poorly kept me close to home, which kept me on track to my bigger goals. I knew lots of kids my age who went away to college and struggled with those newfound freedoms in ways I didn't. Frankly, having parties and alcohol around me all the time, in my own home, made that way of life far less appealing. For me, there was no mystery to explore. I saw firsthand what I didn't want my life to become. I saw adults acting in ways I never wanted to, in ways I would not want to emulate.

Academically, I got my general education requirements over with, using a less expensive option, so I could transfer to the four-year college of my choosing, which was a far better choice than the one I'd had two years prior. In fact, I eventually received letters of acceptance from universities that I never thought would even consider me. By going to a junior college, I also got the less expensive opportunity to try out different courses of study, which had me transitioning from a business focus to creative writing focus. In all, being delayed in attending a four-year university was the best thing for me, though I wouldn't have believed it at the time I received my rejection letters.

Think of Joseph in the Old Testament. Surely, he must have thought that being his father's favorite would allow him every conceivable privilege his father, Jacob, could afford, like the richly ornamented coat his father had given him. Don't you think Joseph must have thought the coat was just the beginning of many advantages of being his father's favorite son? As he pranced around in that coat, I'm sure he thought there would be even more bounty like that to come. Well, what a surprise party his brothers had waiting for him when they threw him into a cistern and sold him into slavery for a mere twenty shekels!

Whatever his expectations were, we hear little of it from Joseph. Unlike me, he never seems to give into bitterness, frustration, or despair. Through all accounts, he is steadfast to his commission to do God's will. We never see him complain, or uphold resentment with acts unbefitting a disciple of God. When Joseph goes into Potiphar's house as a slave, the Lord God is with him even there and God blesses Joseph's faithful heart and character. Eventually, "His master saw that the Lord was with him and that the Lord gave him success in everything he did, Joseph found favor in his eyes and became his attendant. Potiphar put him in charge of his household, and he entrusted to his care everything he owned. From the time he put him in charge of his household and of all that he owned, the Lord blessed the household of the Egyptian because of Joseph. The blessing of the Lord was on everything Potiphar had, both in the house and in the field. So he left in Joseph's care everything he had" (Genesis 39:3–6).

Even as Joseph is wrongly accused of an affair with Potiphar's wife and put into the dungeon to serve his punishment, Joseph turns lemons into lemonade. We are told that even in prison, God is with Joseph: "The Lord was with him; he showed him kindness and granted him favor in the eyes of the prison warden. So the warden put Joseph in charge of all those held in the prison, and he was made responsible for all that was done there. The warden paid no attention to anything under Joseph's care, because the Lord was with Joseph and gave him success in whatever he did" (Genesis 39:21–23).

I have long thought about Joseph and I have concluded that it is not as much God's favor that sets Joseph apart from every other person who has faced disappointment; it is Joseph's faithfulness to God in the midst of disappointment that sets him apart. Consider numerous passages in the New Testament that rely both on the supernatural ability of God and a person's personal faith to alleviate a burden, physical ailment, or sin. Continually, Jesus and his disciples encouraged the sickly and sinfully downtrodden to acknowledge that faith would set them free (Matthew 9:22; Matthew 15:28; Acts 14:9; Acts 26:18)—free from either a life of sin, as with the woman at the well, or free from physical impairment, as with the woman who had bled for several years without cure.

What is also clear is that it is not necessarily faith in the idea that our circumstances will eventually turn in our favor that saves us, but it is the faith in Christ that saves us. If we believe in hopes and dreams more than we believe in Christ, we walk the fine line of the prosperity gospel, which is not an accurate depiction of the Bible. Our faith must rely solely on Christ. Faith should be grounded in the character of Christ, and the fact that the Lord God loves us, regardless of whether or not we get what we want. Consider how great a parent's love is for their child, but seldom does a child—a mature, disciplined child—get everything he or she longs for.

Being committed to God, as Joseph was, has absolutely nothing to do with our circumstances—it has to do with our character and faithful submission to God. I know this idea firsthand, as I struggled to make sense out of six miscarriages. By the fifth miscarriage, I was furious at God and my own physical inability to have a child. That I could not do what many ill-equipped teenage girls could do was disheartening, to say the least. By the sixth time I miscarried, God had moved in me supernaturally and I had submitted to him in a way I never had before.

I saw that, contrary to my inner beliefs, I was not in charge of my destiny: I could not eat better or work out more to attain the perfect body for childbearing. If that last baby were to come, it would be by God's mighty hands. If you or someone you know has struggled with infertility, you know what I'm talking about. So, by the sixth miscarriage (my eighth pregnancy in all, since I had given birth to two children during this time), I knew God wanted the best for me—whatever that was. I had to submit to His plan, rather than my own, and in doing so, I gained strength and an overwhelming peace that I'd never had before.

It's clear that our failures matter, but mostly they matter only to us. What looks like failure is usually just another opportunity for God to reveal Himself in a mighty way; God can turn tragedy and disappointment into a happy ending. Staying grounded on the Rock, which is God, keeps us away from temptations such as envy, bitterness, and hate while we go through these trying and tiring disappointments.

Though sections of Joseph's story have been included here, turn to Genesis 37 to see how else God speaks to you in these portions of Scripture.

Surprise! You're Going to Fail!—Bible Study

1. What attitude did Joseph have toward his brothers that may have incited their anger and jealousy? Have you ever had a prideful attitude toward others that God might have wanted shaken out, so that you could more aptly glorify Him?

2. Consider the verse: "It is for discipline that you endure; God deals with you as with sons; for what son is there whom his father does not discipline?" (Hebrews 12:7). How does this verse comfort you when you realize that God may have been disciplining you when you faced disappointment, so that the end result—your Christ-like maturity—would be more well developed in the future?

3. What has been the greatest disappointment of your life?

4. Was this disappointment your doing, or someone else's? Have you forgiven that other person? Have you forgiven yourself? Have you forgiven God?

5. In terms of disappointments, how would your life be different had those disappointments turned out the way you had planned? Do you see how God intervened to reveal a better plan? I know this can be difficult in terms of long-term, lifelong disappointments, such as terminal illness, infertility, or the earlier-than-expected loss of a loved one, but has God brought any blessing or revelation to you even in light of such heavy burdens? Have you been able to bring life-giving comfort to someone else because of your gained experience? Could you now?

6. Considering your ability to deal with disappointment, how would you like to be more like Joseph? What would you commit to doing to become more like Joseph?

Chasing Elvis

"We know that there is no such thing as an idol in the world,
and that there is no God but one."
1 Corinthians 8:4

We went to Graceland the year after Elvis died. We actually drove our boxy white Winnebago on the cross-country trek all the way from California to Tennessee. We did not have air-conditioning in that motorhome, so if you live in the mostly temperate part of Northern California, as we did, this sort of heat could be quite daunting.

In Arizona my memory still holds the scars from green, oozy liquid shooting out of the motorhome's radiator onto sizzling black pavement. It was as though hell was closer to the surface and there was no worry of it ever freezing over. My other distinct memory of Arizona was that of my brother, Keith, passing out after leaving a roadside diner. First, he had turned a greenish white, staggered a little toward the motorhome, and then bumbled around the dented bumper of a random pickup truck. His long, skinny arms seemed to lose their freckly color right before he muttered something incomprehensible to my father. He then wrinkled up like a badly crafted piece of origami and fell to the ground in a heap.

We stayed—from California to Tennessee—in campgrounds, usually KOA campgrounds where we would either get along with, or fight with, kids we'd meet in swamp-coolered, fake-wood-paneled game rooms. These "game rooms" usually consisted of one or two pinball machines, a battle-scarred pool table, one quasi-usable pool stick, and three kids who appeared to spend most of their school days in detention or Juvenile Hall.

Once in the basic vicinity of Graceland, it became obvious that Elvis and his death were a booming business. Parking across a steaming and dirty street, we dodged traffic to find ourselves outside the ornate gates of the King's house. My mother ran her slender, long fingers over the bricks of Elvis's high brick fence where visitors had written tearful farewell thoughts in black Sharpie pen. My mother's eyes began to get misty, like the water bubbling on a tabletop fountain at the check-in desk of a KOA campground.

Slowly, as though she'd played out in her mind what mourning Elvis should look like, she walked solemnly up the gently winding driveway to the rear of Elvis's home. The main house was not yet open for tours, but it did not matter because here at his gravesite my mother cried, clinging to the black wrought iron railing in front of Elvis's rather enormous tombstone. Her nose was red and her large butterfly glasses hid her tear-filled red eyes. Still, she looked pretty in her purple shirt, cut-off jean shorts, and sad face.

Always the clown, my brother clung to the wrought iron behind her, made a ridiculous face of intense sadness, looked up to the sky with his hands punctuating upward, as if to say, "Why? Why?" and then dropped his head, as though overtaken by overwhelmingly distraught emotion. As his head bobbed with artificial sobs, I began to laugh at the pantomime. Without missing a tear, my mother's head seemed to

144

turn completely around on her long, graceful neck. She shot a look that quickly reduced us to more appropriate somberness.

Now, one would think after a few minutes of standing staring at a tombstone, you would casually walk away, but no. My mother seemed to be ruminating on the tombstone. She was parked there. In fact, the line of tombstone gazers was backing up because my mother had become a roadblock. She was the broken-down tow-truck that would not move. Keith and I had tucked ourselves away under some hanging vines near a large, ornate garden fountain dedicated to Elvis's mother, Gladys, but we could see that my mother was going to have to be moved by something other than her own will. Eventually, seeing the traffic jam, my father went to her. Startled by his touch, she allowed him to take her arm in his as he led her away.

I always assumed that my mother had a predetermined time in her head for mourning at gravesites, or even sitting in hospital rooms visiting dying people. When we visited either one, as we did on vacations and idle days, she spent an exceedingly long time crying and carrying on, regardless of who the person was, or how long they'd been dead or ill. She could wail and cry as loudly for someone who'd been dead ten years as for someone dead ten minutes; it made no difference. At a gravesite, she would sprawl out right on top of the grass, lying prostrate in front of the tombstone, crying inconsolably until it became quite unbearable to watch.

Combing the obituary section of the newspaper could result in ruining an entire day if she could find even the slightest connections to any deceased person. One time, she found someone with my name who had died. It ruined an entire Saturday and she cried for the dead woman as though they'd actually known each other. The more information in the obituary, the more she mourned.

With enough time spent at Elvis's strangely misspelled headstone, we began to entertain the thought of leaving. That's when my mother saw Vester. As she rushed toward Elvis's Uncle Vester at the guard shack, flip-flops smacking the hot, muggy Memphis ground, I was sure my mother had finally lost it. As though she'd known Uncle Vester her entire life, she asked about Lisa Marie and Priscilla. The old, gray-haired man seemed relieved that someone cared about the welfare of his family. And, frankly, he seemed pleased that someone knew him: he talked with my mom at great length. My dad rolled his eyes, but didn't dare let my mother see. My brother and I tried hard to retain a respectable air: In a relatively short amount of time we had perfected the art of looking sadly at the ground, shaking our heads, nodding slowly, and looking up at the sky with determined resoluteness to find the answers to Elvis's tragic, senseless death.

At times like these, I always had an internal conversation going on inside my head that went something like this: We have driven thousands of miles to see a man we will never meet, who didn't know us, who did nothing for us, and yet, we've spent our entire vacation to see where he used to live, so that we can now stand and visit with a distant relative that Elvis probably didn't even know existed. All I know is that if we don't go get a slushy to cool down our inner cores, I think we're all going to meet the same fate as the egg I plopped into the microwave last week. On the outside though, I stood there respectfully nodding at every absurd detail Vester chose to throw at my mother.

Years later, when I was in my senior year in college, I got a fictional writing assignment, but I procrastinated on that paper. Instead, I pulled from this real experience for my topic. Red pens in hand, all the students and the professor critiqued my paper through pursed lips and squinted eyes, and the professor concluded that the character of the mother was too unrealistic.

"No one would ever know Elvis's Uncle Vester," he said analytically.

This is where I wanted to sit back, put my feet up on the table, light a cigar, put my hands up in the air and say, "Amen, brother." Instead

I said, coughing a little to clear my throat, "Well, I know this was a fictional assignment, but I actually chose to write about something in my own life experience." I cleared my throat again, and felt the weight of all eyes zeroing in on me, as though it was all making sense now.

Someone from a study group had already told me that I was an anomaly, having come from a blue-collared background; statistically, I shouldn't even be in college. I always wondered where my bare feet were supposed to have landed, and how many kids were supposed to have been tugging on my tattered apron. Yes, according to that assessment I suppose I should have been barefoot and pregnant somewhere, but instead, here I was in a senior seminar class trying to explain my Graceland experience with my "unrealistic" mother.

"And," I continued to croak out, "that unrealistic character," I paused, "is in fact my mother."

There was a gasp of disbelief. Some students put their hands to their mouths and their eyes narrowed at me, as if to say, "White-trash, leave now and no one will get hurt."

"And," I continued, "she did indeed know Uncle Vester." I wanted to add, "And if you think that's unrealistic, you don't know the half of it."

My mother's infatuation with Elvis, and her preoccupation in worshipping him did not always confound me. Growing up with idolatry of that sort becomes a comfortable thing at an early age. I think most of us don't even think twice about people worship because society, at large, worships those who are held in high esteem by their purported celebrity or sports status.

With that said, after Elvis died and my mother's deep-felt connection to Elvis played out in a number of strange ways, I saw how frivolous and wasted her time was. The time she spent distracted by someone virtually unreal, and very much untouchable, could have been expended on working out her deep-seated insecurities and hurts, and used to realize God's overwhelming forgiveness and love for her. Unfortunately, the things my mother chased after were oftentimes the things that offered only instantaneous, temporary fulfillment. When you seek things with such fleeting sustenance, you must seek those things continually, because there is always a void, always a hole, and always a hollow feeling where something satisfying should be.

Regarding idolatry, Merriam-Webster's dictionary defines it as "the worship of a physical object as a god," or "the immoderate attachment or devotion to something." Though most people don't consider themselves idolaters, there is usually someone or something that consumes their time, which takes away from worshipping a perfect and worthy God, something that in comparison to a perfect God falls pitifully short.

One of the biggest problems with worshipping or idolizing people is that we do so based on faulty criteria. Consider this verse:

When they entered, he looked at Eliab and thought, "Surely the Lord's anointed is before Him." But the Lord said to Samuel, "Do not look at his appearance or at the height of his stature, because I have rejected him; for God sees not as man sees, for man looks at the outward appearance, but the Lord looks at the heart (1 Samuel 16:6–7).

Who else besides God can look at a man's heart? So, regardless of how endearing or charismatic a person is, they are still only human, and "human" has proven to be repetitively incapable of sustaining eternal perfection or adoration.

Think of how often you have heard someone speak ill of someone they once worshipped. A wife turning on her husband; a child turning on his or her parent, or fans turning on their team. How many times does affection and admiration turn to unmerciful criticism and negativity when someone in high status does not perform as he or she was expected to? When we idolize those who were faulty from the start, it shouldn't surprise us when they stumble and fall, and yet that very thing fills gossip magazines.

Aside from the inevitable disappointment in worshipping fallible people, just think of the burden those people have to bear when faced with the unrelenting scrutiny. Physically attractive women struggle incessantly with self-esteem issues, while men flounder with the necessity to appear successful and wealthy. I surmise that that is why a number of celebrities struggle with their fame to such a great extent. It is hard to continually please an indecisive world that elevates you beyond your aptitude.

Frankly, nothing has been more sobering for me regarding idolatry than exploring the wonders of God. Yes, seeing someone dance and sing is entertaining and can fill an evening with a lot of enjoyment, but looking at a Rainbow Jellyfish that appears to light up, and pondering the mind that made such a thing is worthy of my time and worship. If you want to idolize something, study the universe and its great expanse and how little we still know about it. To me, that is worthy of worship. A friend of mine said she recently read a book on quantum physics in order to get a better glimpse of God and when she was done, she was even more in awe of Him.

Though the accomplishments of men and women are notable, the overwhelming sense one should have is that of pure reverence for the fact that God made everything. It says in Psalm 19 that "The heavens declare the glory of God; the skies proclaim the work of his hands. Day after day they pour forth speech; night after night they display knowledge." There is no inconsistency in what God has made. His creation proves itself every day and every night. Scientists now find that even parts of the universe and our world that seem chaotic have logic behind them. It takes an incredibly obstinate person to give accolades to a person for things that will deteriorate and fade away but not be able to give proper reverence and glory to God for the days that pass without question, uncertainty, or doubt.

No one knew this like Moses: God revealed himself again and again, for forty years to be exact, as the Israelites wandered the desert, and yet with God's presence still lingering in the air—either by pillar of fire or pillar of smoke—the Israelites continued to turn from reverence to God to the formation of idols they crafted from their own imaginations and hands. About this, God said, "You shall not make for yourself an idol in the form of anything in heaven above or on the earth beneath or in the waters below" (Deuteronomy 5:8). Why would God care, if He already knew that He was in charge? Why would He care? Well, He addresses that in Deuteronomy 4:16. God tells the people of Israel, "So that you do not become corrupt and make for yourselves an idol, an image of any shape, whether formed like a man or a woman." Just as human beings perverted the Garden of Eden with insatiable covetousness, God knew we could corrupt worship too. Instead of worshipping holy and good, man's worship can easily turn toward that which is questionable and vile. God knew what He was doing when He instructed us to worship only Him, because we would "become corrupt," by worshipping anything else.

With the imprint of commonality we all have stamped upon our beings, we long to worship something: it is innately within us. Missionaries and explorers have found this phenomenon in the darkest jungles, as tribesmen worship nature, animals, and all the awe-inspiring things they see. In the hallowed halls of ivy-league universities, this phenomenon is no different, just fixated on the superiority of sterilized academia. What is perplexing about this latter stance is the deliberate removal of God in order to preserve the idolatry of man rather than God. Once, the greatest minds of science were those that revered God: Galileo, Newton, and Agassiz were just a few of the most prominent, radical thinkers of their day who saw science as the obvious outcropping of God's creative genius. These men were not frightened or intimidated to be second best to a God whose intellect superseded their own. It was enough for them to realize that every revelation they encountered brought them one step closer to the throne of God Almighty.

I encourage all of us to be like them, explorers and scientists who look and find reasons to get closer to God, "for since the creation of the world His invisible attributes, His eternal power and divine nature, have been clearly seen, being understood through what has been made, so that ... [we] ... are without excuse" (Romans 1:20). For further understanding on this, read John 5:40–47, and consider the following questions.

Chasing Elvis—Bible Study

1. What idols do you have in your life? (Spouse, children, self, success, money, family, job, education, art collection, sport adoration,
   celebrities, etc.)

2. What is the character of God? Write a list of at least five adjectives
   that are biblically sound.

3. What is the character of man? Write a list of at least five adjectives that are biblically sound. How does man fall short in comparison to God?

4. Why do you think it's easier to worship things/people rather than God?

5. What are some ways you could worship God more completely starting today?

Monument of Love

"As one whom his mother comforts, so I will comfort you."
Isaiah 66:13

I was raised in Oklahoma, California. Never heard of it? Then you've never heard of Bill and Lucy Naoma, my grandparents. I had parents, and for all intents and purposes they raised me, but in those early developmental years, that awake time, I was with my paternal grandparents. My grandmother was from Texas and my grandfather from Oklahoma, so in a sense, I was raised on the Texas-Oklahoma state line, fifty miles south of San Francisco.

My grandparents seamlessly transferred their Okie upbringings into a California setting. They came to California in the forties when the notorious Dust Bowl made farming impossible in Oklahoma. They were poor. This sort of hardship my grandmother went through made her considerably stronger than your average person. I cannot imagine my grandmother having confided her hurt or disappointment in all these things to anyone, and Dr. Phil was not around to tell her that she'd be OK. She was of a steely caliber, not the likes to be found in this day and age, at least not in the continental United States. There are probably women like her in Africa, or Mexico, or South America, but not the United States. I mean, the woman picked cotton while trying to figure out ways to feed her family and care for a handicapped son. The most I've ever picked is lint off a black sweater.

In the small tract-housing development they lived in, it was as though they ignored all modern amenities. Though the lot on which their tiny house sat could not have been larger than 5,000 square feet, they lived as if they had a sprawling farm. My grandfather had built a worm box for fishing, a grain shed for storing the grain for the ducks and rabbits, and a large pen split in two for ducks on the one side, and rabbits on the other. There were four fruit trees and a vegetable garden. There was a larger than usual garden turtle with a missing leg hidden under an old white abandoned refrigerator where my grandpa would store things.

In the duck coop, the ducks would take turns paddling around in a large galvanized water basin. On the other side, the rabbits snuggled close together for warmth in their chicken-wired cage. These animals were not trivial entertainment. In fact, I learned pretty quickly that it was best to have them go unnamed, because from my experience, it is harder to eat Daffy or Fluffy than it is to eat duck or rabbit. And Grandma was always clear about what room I should be in when she went to skin a rabbit because shockingly, and I will assume unbeknownst to most, rabbits make a strange, high-pitched squeal as they are being slaughtered.

A strange result of all that was my grandmother's endearing saying, as she pulled shirts or sweaters over our heads. "Skin a bunny," she would say in a sing-songy way, as my shirt schwooped over and off my head. I still say that to my children to this day, even though I know that the technical aspects of "skinning a bunny" are anything but charming and child-friendly. All of it—bunny skinning, feather plucking, worm-bed building, catfish gutting and scaling, three-legged turtle poking—it was all beautiful. It was the very best of my childhood, and I long for it still.

As a child, all I knew of my grandmother was that she seldom cried, but she wasn't a machine either. She was silently compassionate, keeping deeper thoughts inside because she seemed to know that's where they were safe. She lived a subtle life, not begging for attention or sympathy, but expecting love and respect from those she loved, and not caring much about extraneous people who bothered her rare balance of simplicity.

Unlike my gregarious mother who eagerly invited the Avon Lady in every Saturday to sit for hours talking and buying countless trinkets, my grandmother verbally accosted any solicitor unwise enough to darken her doorstep. I think most salespeople would have been utterly alarmed to know of the .22-caliber rifle behind her door. If my grandma's "Get off my property," comment flung coldly in the shocked faces of salesmen did not move them quickly down her front porch and away from her home, well who can say what she'd have done with that rifle? I only know that my brother and I would tiptoe our fluffy, white towheads over the thin tin bar on the screen door, our fingers uplifting our bodies, while we stared cheerfully at the next unsuspecting salesman, and my grandmother would sometimes say nothing. She'd brush us away from the screen door, while wiping her hands dry on a gingham apron and slam the heavy wooden door in some salesman's face she'd never seen before. It did not matter what they were selling. She did not have time to sit idly talking to strangers about anything.

Grandma was usually busily canning vegetables, or working in her garden, or baking something. It became clear that if my grandmother's hands touched any kind of food, even a former fluffy rabbit, I would eat it happily and revel in the fact that it was superb. She appeared undaunted by normally intimidating tasks. She was fiercely loyal and in

156

love with my grandfather, and most importantly to me, she loved me. I knew she loved me. This woman who did not like very many people and who grew tired of the frivolous nature of most companionship wanted me around, even if it was time spent in total mutual silence. She liked me, and I knew that was exceptional.

I knew she would grow weary of company because sometimes her sister would come visit from Oklahoma, and within a week, my grandmother would be quite ready for her to leave. Aunt Rosie was not entirely pleasant, so I understood. She was the youngest and most indulged girl of three sisters and one boy. My grandmother was the third of the four children, and had never been indulged in anything. My grandmother had actually pulled the plow in their fields, something Rosie would mention often in her visits. "Oh, old Naoma was just as good as a cow when she was home helping Daddy in the fields. Just as good and strong as that old cow we had that one time, weren't cha Big Sister? Oh, what was that cow's name?" She would fade off and flit about in pastel colored chiffon dresses, gazing at her reflection in anything. According to my grandfather, Rosie was her father's pride and sang in the church choirs, and flirted with boys. She must have been very good at flirting with boys, because she parlayed that craft when she was just seventeen, and while babysitting for a man in his fifties, they had an affair that ruined his marriage. Soon after his marriage toppled, they married, and because his children were older than her, they never had children of their own.

When she came to visit, she would bring her accordion and pull it out of a dark leather case lined with bright royal velvet. She would hum a bit to get her melody and then begin, "What a friend we have in Jeee—sus . . ." Her voice was high and shrill, but my grandmother's gentle voice was soft and low, barely audible. If ever my grandmother's voice got above a whisper, Rosie would chastise her, "Naomie, you just need to be more quiet, Sweetheart. You know you can't sing, Big

Sissy." A southern accent can say almost anything and sound like honey sliding over a spoonful of sugar, almost. I wanted to terrorize Rosie by poking holes in the papery bellows of her accordion with a sharpened lead pencil, but it was not really in my nature to step out of obedience. Being appropriately chastised, my grandmother would always fall into line. She had been stung so often by this hornet southern belle; she didn't even know how to dodge them. When Rosie would finally leave after what seemed like months instead of days, it was like sighing into a big, comfy, overstuffed chair.

I believed I was my grandmother's favorite, though to have said that to me would have been an expression of more emotion than she was comfortable with. This was important to me because my brother was usually everyone's favorite. But I knew that being loved by someone like my grandmother was like leaning back on the edge of the Grand Canyon, falling with your eyes closed tight, and knowing with utmost certainty that you'd inexplicably land in a soft place.

My grandmother did not buy me lots of things. In fact, she was painfully frugal: one might even venture to say she was cheap. She could squeeze a penny until it yelped. Often we drove to town to go to the pharmacy in my grandparents' large 1966 white Chevy Impala. It was pristine, like everything they owned—not the best, but pristine. I would roll around on the floorboard of that car, running my fingers over relief of astrological signs on the black floor-mats, or I would sit in the large, vacuous backseat and play with the speaker in the center of the seat with the gold emblem of an impala on it. Mostly, I took in the smell of the black leather seats and listened to the melodic blinking of the turn signal and the clicking of my grandmother's simple gold band against the big black steering wheel.

When we arrived at the pharmacy, it didn't matter if a week had passed or a month, my grandmother would take me slowly but directly to the counter and show the pharmacist how much I'd grown. He and his female assistant always said I was just getting prettier and prettier. Good answer, because my grandmother would have taken nothing less than hearing that I was wholly perfect. After being commended for my rapid growth, I'd meander around the store and fawn over the birthday figurines of the little girls with big full skirts holding birthstone flowers. I know I never failed to mention how badly I wanted one. In fact, though I'd like to think I used politeness and decorum, I'll bet I was pretty pesky about it. My grandmother never gave in. "Shelly," she'd say, "Put those down before you break one." She was not frivolous enough to cave to the whimpering and begging of a child, even her favorite child.

Finally, one birthday on the middle of their polished kitchen table sat a perfect white cube of a box. Wiggling the lid from the box, I suspected what might lie in the middle of all that crisp white tissue paper, and I was right: a birthday figurine. She had brown hair and an ivory dress of glass with red flowers strewn about. She held a blue flower with my birthstone in the middle. With that, I knew that to my grandmother I was something else.

In the afternoons, I would take naps in my grandmother's sewing room. Sunshine glowed on the other side of my grandmother's golden curtains and reflected strands of sunlight onto the white walls of her sewing room. I wanted to hold onto that feeling of the soft sheets both cool and warm at the same time, making a safe cocoon around my body. At four years old, I already knew the value of holding onto such things, of breathing them in heavily and deeply before they wafted away, like the moist brief mist of crashing waves against cold, dark, edgy rocks. I will never forget lying there, drifting off to sleep and wishing that I could be there forever—that my time with my grandmother would never end. It is always with a lump in my throat that I think of my grandma.

Sometimes God gives us the wonderful opportunity to have restful places and times. The times I spent with my grandparents were the most peaceful times of my life. There was something special about knowing what to expect, and experiencing the expected. That sounds ludicrous unless you know that my parents, just eighteen and nineteen when they married, had their own tumultuous problems in raising young children and adjusting their youth to the demands and burdens that come with marriage.

Oftentimes, my parents' arguing and physical fights were very frightening to me. I was a shy, quiet child, and their explosions would incite worry and anxiety in me that was difficult to manage. It was not unusual to lie awake nearly an entire night, worrying about what might happen between them. For the difficulties outside our home, such as school or squabbles with friends, I worried twice as much. Anything that might perchance bring about a difficult, problematic, or troubling situation would cause me to worry until my chest would tighten and my head would whirl. As a small child I had a hard time coping, but my grandparents—on both sides of my family—were always a refreshing source of escape. What made my paternal grandmother special was her delight in me. She saw in me something worthy, something few people probably saw because of my quirky timidity.

My grandmother encouraged me in my pursuits. In fact, both of my grandmothers encouraged my pursuits. Being artistic, they would buy me paper and pens and suggest things for me to draw. They would talk about my drawings and ask me to draw specific pictures for them. Sometimes they would even frame and hang my drawings in visible places. What makes that sort of relationship special is that they had to know me, in order to encourage my interests. If they had encouraged me to sing loudly for an audience, I would have resisted them and known that they did not have my interest in mind, and it would have been obvious they didn't know about me, or care to know me.

What makes anything special is the way it pleases our individual souls. For me, being in relationship with someone on an intimate level is special, being appeased on a level with the masses, not so special. I think God knows that and oftentimes, He will orchestrate those dear, meaningful relationships to reflect His purpose to please us on an intimate level.

When the individuality of our soul seeks a specific need for the enrichment of our intimate character, sometimes God brings it to us unexpectedly and without our asking. Just as the "Spirit helps us in our weakness [when] we don't know what we ought to pray for . . . the Spirit himself intercedes for us with groans that words cannot express. And he who searches our hearts knows the mind of the Spirit, because the Spirit intercedes for the saints in accordance with God's will" (Romans 8:26–27).

It was most certainly God's will that my grandmother bestow uninterrupted time, affection, and even favoritism on me. Though I didn't know it then, I would need it later, like an explorer in the wilderness with multiple canteens of water that would have first seemed an unnecessary burden. With my grandmother, I drank in every drop of her love and care, and in my darkest moments I pulled from those cherished memories to find that I was worthy of love, time, and effort.

We are needy people who have needs that oftentimes get met without request or begging because we aren't even cognizant of what we need, but God is, and "the lamp of the Lord searches the spirit of a man; it searches out his inmost being" (Proverbs 20:27), and provides accordingly. It is being given some blessing that stands as a signpost that God is ever-present and aware of your innermost being.

In the Bible, God has the Israelites take twelve stones from the middle of the Jordan River to establish a memorial that will be for "the people of Israel forever" (Joshua 4:7b). My thinking on this is that when God wants you to remember something "forever," it's probably something worth remembering.

The building of this memorial comes at a pivotal time in the wanderings of the Israelites. Their leader, Moses, has just died after having led them for forty years through the desert, God is in the process of leading them over the Jordan River to the Promised Land, the land of "milk and honey" via their new leader, Joshua, and it is the culmination of God having provided for them and sustaining them for forty long years.

God knows the mind of man can oftentimes be his own worst enemy. As a child, it was the strangeness of new situations that made me anxious, not the situations themselves. Oftentimes, once I was engaged in the new situation I was fine, but the fear leading up to it could be overwhelming. I still remind myself that "there is no fear in love. But perfect love drives out fear, because fear has to do with punishment," and through Christ we are forgiven rather than punished (1 John 4:18).

With the example of how God instructed the Israelites to set up monuments for memoriam that would last forever, we too, should be reminded to set our minds upon our own memorials that prove God's provision and sustenance in times of difficulty. Don't just rely on your mental capacity to contain all the various ways God has provided, make a physical reminder that will withstand times of doubt, fear, and anxiety. I suggest keeping a blessings journal that attests to the provisions of God. While it would never be easy for me to forget the gracious nature of my grandmother, it is far easier to forget some other lesser but no less significant way that God has provided for me over my lifetime.

Read the following passage, and then answer the questions that follow.

"When you have crossed the Jordan into the land the Lord your God is giving you, set up some large stones and coat them with plaster. Write on them all the words of this law when you have crossed over to enter the land the Lord your God is giving you, a land flowing with milk and honey, just as the Lord, the God of your fathers, promised you. And when you have crossed the Jordan, set up these stones on Mount Ebal, as I command you today, and coat them with plaster. Build there an altar to the Lord your God, an altar of stones. Do not use any iron tool upon them. Build the altar of the Lord your God with fieldstones and offer burnt offerings on it to the Lord your God. Sacrifice fellowship offerings there, eating them and rejoicing in the presence of the Lord your God. And you shall write very clearly all the words of this law on these stones you have set up." Deuteronomy 27:2–8

Monument of Love—Bible Study

1. Why do you think God had the Israelites set up this monument?

2. Why do you think He had them set it up before they entered the "land flowing with milk and honey"?

3. If they hadn't been reminded of how God had provided in the past, what might they have done in good times?

4. What are some ways God has provided for you in difficult times?

5. How has He provided for you in good times?

6. Is it easier for you to see God's presence in good times or bad times? Many people say it's harder for them to acknowledge God in good times because they take the credit for good times themselves. Do you have a tendency to do this?

7. If you have a tendency to do this, can you see why God who desires to have a close, intimate relationship with you might allow bad times?

8. What is the plaster-covered stone that you will commit to setting up to remember God's provisions for you? If you have children, what can you encourage them to do today to acknowledge God's provisions for them, so they don't take God for granted as they live in the "land of milk and honey"?

Rumble in the Desert

"A hot-tempered man stirs up strife, But the slow to anger calms a dispute."
Proverbs 15:18

When I was about nine years old, my dad's best friend, Albert, killed a man in Montana . . . well, he allegedly killed a man in Montana, and though Albert had always been a part of our lives, he moved even further west and became an even bigger, scarier part of our lives. In the fall of 1975, we went to Nevada for my dad's yearly deer hunting trip, and just like clockwork, my dad's best friend joined us.

First of all, let me say that the rumor of Albert killing the man in Montana was going around our intertwined families and spreading like wildfire. My grandmother was certain he'd done it. My grandfather was convinced. In lengthy sordid details, my grandfather told of Albert's mischievous, undisciplined teenage years. Together, my grandparents conjured up every miniscule recollection to seal the deal, at least in their minds. And, given their long history as close friends, my father was also pretty convinced Albert had done the alleged crime. So, as you can imagine, the yearly hunting trip that my family and Albert usually scheduled to spend together was one of those situations my father thought best avoided. In my dad's best attempt to elude Albert, my father told him we'd be hunting in one area of Nevada, while in reality, we went to a completely different location.

Well, Albert must have suspected such a thing. While we were setting up our camp equipment on the edge of an eerie dessert with not one living creature, far off in the distance came a bouncing RV with a trail of dust billowing out behind it: it was Albert. Though my dad had apparently chosen an abandoned military test site for our hunting trip, Albert must have sniffed the air, examined broken twigs, and scrutinized droppings from forest animals to assess and determine our exact location on the Nevada map. It was stunning.

The reasons my father chose to elude Albert are, of course, pure speculation, but from the moment he saw Albert coming toward us across the deserted Nevada landscape, my dad seemed to begin a low, slow sweat that did not cease until they parted ways. I'm pretty sure that one single trip spent with the suspected killer decreased my father's overall lifespan by at least 3.2 years. You see, what my father surely realized was that when mixed together, Albert and my mother were an ominous concoction. Like two asteroids set on a collision course from the beginning of time, they would come together in the dark expanse of the universe, and in a collision of obstinate opinions and wills they would often bring forth a bewildering and fascinating explosion of impassioned fury.

With each meeting, there was the cordial prologue: each opponent sizing the other up. In some ways, it was like two sumo wrestlers circling right before some earth-shaking leap across an imaginary boundary. I must say that Albert appeared to take immense pleasure in inciting my mother to anger and pure exasperation. As I remember, he ignited that in most people, but when my mother had been drinking, it was worse—much worse.

Typically, my mother was not a happy drunk. At first, she was sad and she would cry a lot. I didn't mind it. I felt like she must have needed to get it out, since she didn't go to a therapist. In her sadness, she would grow melancholy, rehashing horrible details of her calamitous childhood, but should someone, some complete and utter dope enter the picture with his pokey stick to taunt the tiger, she would unleash an attack on that fool that would leave a small village digging through rubble for days.

As for Albert, he was a large man, a really large man. He weighed around four hundred pounds and since his first wife had shot him in the back, he was paralyzed from the waist down and confined to a wheelchair. She, his first wife, Helen, had shot him one crisp fall Sunday morning as they were getting ready to go to church. I had always thought it was strange that they would have made that small pitiful effort to go to church when clearly God's word had not penetrated either of them. He had hit her and she refused to take one more instance of his abuse. As he stood in the sun-bathed yellow kitchen and poured himself coffee, she pulled the trigger on a handgun, and he fell over, collapsing to the ground. That was the last day Albert would ever stand upright.

As for Helen, she was convicted and sentenced to twenty-five years in jail. It was the end to a terrifying and abusive marriage. My parents had said that Helen was crazy, though having met and spent time with Albert, I wondered if he had been able to drive her to such insanity. My mother said that one day while Albert and Helen dined at their house, an argument erupted between them, in which Helen furiously stormed off. She actually began to walk home, a fifteen mile distance from my parent's house to theirs.

My mother said they waited, thinking that Helen had simply taken a break to walk around the block and cool off, but as an hour passed they realized that she was not returning. Eventually, they piled into the car to find her and pick her up. My mother said they were surprised to find her almost home, still walking at a hurried pace. As they pulled slowly up to her side, my mother said she was horrified to see that Helen's large, weighty legs had rubbed together in such heat and friction that they were bloody. Helen seemed to be completely unaware that blood was rapidly streaming down her legs, making her light cotton voile dress tacky and stuck to her white bloodied skin. Given that story, Helen seemed crazy, but thankfully, not every crazy person shoots his or her spouse.

Albert was uncharacteristically mean, like a made-up character. Sometimes you cannot make up such things, they just are. My dad liked to tell the story about how when he and Albert were eighteen, Albert got drunk and dove into the ocean just as the tide receded, and he broke his neck. In the days that followed, my dad said Albert's face and neck turned black and blue. His eyes were just slits in the puffiness of his round tender face. Everyone prodded him to go to the hospital, but stubbornly he refused. Finally, the throbbing pain overtook his orneriness and weeks after the incident, he finally conceded and got the medical attention he needed.

I think all of the other stories attesting to Albert's overall meanness now paled in comparison to the one about him allegedly killing a man. All that was known was that the man had been one of Albert's neighbors. Apparently, they had had a long-standing disagreement about things that territorial neighbors tend to argue about. Then, out of the blue, the man disappeared. One week led to another and no one had seen or heard from him. Like an exhaled breath, he was gone. After five weeks, he literally popped up in an isolated waterway. His bloated water-logged body surfaced and drifted ashore. His arms had been bound with rope and bricks. Coincidentally, those same rope and bricks were found to be missing from Albert's backyard.

170

The mounds of evidence also showed that on the same day authorities suspected Albert of killing the man, Albert had driven across the border of Montana into Wyoming. There, he visited every relative he'd ever known. At one stop, Albert asked an elderly relative if he could wash the truck with the old gray-haired man's hose. Wheeling out into the heat of the summer sun across the gravel in his wheelchair, he aimed the hose into the back of his truck and let the stream wash away dust and blood. He turned to the old man. "Killed a hog and that blood just won't come out," he explained. The old man nodded. "You got a broom and some soap?" The man poured dripping dish soap over the bed of the truck and Albert scrubbed with the tattered ends of a wheat-colored broom until the bed of the truck was sparkling clean.

The authorities went after Albert with a vengeance, for the evidence was clear, but how could a handicapped man in a wheelchair do such a thing? How? The evidence could not explain everything, though I myself had seen Albert shoot a coyote on the run out of his car window with his right or left hand in one clean shot, leaving the red furry animal tumbling to a dusty halt. And, the evidence had not considered the fact that the missing neighbor had been going through an acrimonious divorce and custody battle, which involved its own list of nefarious characters. No, Albert was free and the rumor wafting through my family, especially from my story-telling grandfather, was that he had gotten away with murder—premeditated, savage, unmerciful murder.

With his freedom in tow, Albert left Montana and headed for the wild west of Nevada. It was with this knowledge that my dad pow-wowed with my mother in the motorhome after Albert arrived at our campsite.

He whispered to my mother, "Now, Lena do not get him angry." Somber-faced, she nodded excitedly. I mean, only an idiot would consider getting in an argument with a loose-cannoned killer, but my mother had not had her first drink of the night yet. "I mean it, Lena. Do not make him mad."

She agreed that she would not argue with him. "Of course, of course," she consoled my father. "I mean, be serious, Jack. You think I don't know how to act?"

As night fell, we sat around the fire and the brandy flowed between the snapping yellow and orange flames. Albert seemed to be hitting on every topic that might incite my mother.

"I got Elvis's new album," he huffed. "What's wrong with him? Sounds just like every other thing he's done . . . horrible." He laughed a little. "I think I could do better than that!" he continued. "You know the problem, he has no range . . ."

My dad appeared to have stopped breathing, but my beautiful mother with her tanned skin and broad, bright smile just responded cheerily, "Gosh, I don't know what you're talking about. I loved it. Oh well, looks like we just have different taste." My mother had become Doris Day.

"Think they'll trade Kenny Stabler?" he prodded.

Oh no, now he's going after the Oakland Raiders—my mother's favorite football team. When will it stop? I thought. Still, my vibrant mother was a pillar of strength.

He continued, "Humph, Kenny Stabler . . . I tell you what—I've always loved the Pittsburg Steelers. Now, that's a team! Completely unlike that Joke-land Raider mess you like so much." He glared at my unwavering mother through the snaps of campfire.

Doris Day responded with a shrug. "Can I get anyone anything? Something to drink? Some marshmallows? Shelly? Keith? You kids want some marshmallows?" I was beginning to like Doris. She was super-friendly and so accommodating.

"Sure," my brother and I responded.

Then, almost as though it was Albert's last hope, he said, "I tell you . . . that Frazier-Ali fight . . . that was the best fight Ali ever fought."

Doris readjusted herself in her creaky camp chair. "You know," she began, "I love Muhammad Ali—you know I do—but he should not have won that fight, no way."

I did not look at him, but I'm sure my dad must have wished he had known how to pray the Rosary, as the tide began to change.

Albert had thrown out the line and the fish had bitten. "Well, I don't know . . . no sensible person would think the way you do." Albert pulled himself more upright in his wheelchair: The joust had begun. "Everyone with half a brain could see that Muhammad Ali was in better shape. I mean, he was just better overall!"

"Hey, Mom," I chirped, "what about those marshmallows?"

"They're in the cabinet above the stove," she snapped. "You know," she began, "Frazier was in way better shape. He completely dominated in most every round and though I love Ali, I really do, always have, he was not in his best form . . . he just wasn't!"

Even I was praying that my mother's mouth would stop making sounds.

"Well," Albert persisted, "who's right? You or the officials who said he won?" He let out a snarling laugh, which was his characteristic taunt—a calling card of sorts.

Oh my Lord, we are going to die in the desert because of a stupid Muhammad Ali fight. Lord, if you're up there, stop her. Stop her now!

My dad let out a deep and throaty cough, as though to remind my mother of what they'd discussed earlier, but she continued, "Albert, you don't know what you're talking about. In fact, you have removed all doubt tonight that you know anything at all. First of all, you aren't good enough to sing to Elvis's houseplants, and Kenny Stabler, he's a simply amazing player on a simply amazing team, and for the record," she threw back her head and finished off the rest of her brandy, "Frazier won that fight!"

"Well," Albert said gruffly, shifting his behemoth body in the sturdy leather seat of his wheelchair, "You'd have to be an idiot to not see that Muhammad Ali was the best fighter, and in the best shape ever in that fight." He shifted again, as my mother's jaw grew tense. "And, you're a fool if you, uh . . ." he hedged for a moment, as if to gain momentum, and hacked something up from his gut to his mouth, which he quickly spit out into the darkness, ". . . if you didn't see it like me and the rest of the world." He resettled into his chair, drawing back his face into the round folds of triple chins, and waited for my mother's response.

"Albert," said my mother, her beautiful eyes ablaze with the glare of the raging fire, "the only fool around here is you, and you're an idiot if you didn't see that Joe Frazier really won that fight, fair and square. They gave that fight to Muhammed Ali because he's a crowd favorite, not because he won it!"

Albert laughed again, provokingly. "Yep." He leaned on one chubby arm, letting the leather and metal of his wheelchair hold him up. "I told Jack you weren't very bright when you first met." He chuckled almost to himself. "I was right then and I'm right now."

I was sure my dad was having a coronary by now, but I refrained from looking at him. I had no defibrillator paddles to offer him anyway. The argument continued until my mother rose from her rickety little camp chair and yelled a few choice expletives into the dark expanse of night. Had there been any living animals around that the nuclear test site hadn't already killed off, it would have probably awoken them from their night slumber, or scared them from their nighttime excursions. Then, trembling with anger, my mother stood at the edge of the fire. She threw her brandy snifter into the fire, letting the glass crash into shards, and marched into the motorhome, slamming the door behind

174

her.

My brother, my dad, and I continued to sit with Albert around the snapping fire in complete silence. So, this is how it's going to end? No one will even find our bodies out here. Well, at least our dead bodies won't be ravaged by animals, since there aren't any. The stories of how Albert had run over his own hunting dogs for not performing well ran clearly through my mind. If he does that to something that he's had since its cute puppy-ness, what does he do to the fiery wife and children of a best friend who tried to lose him in the Nevadan desert?

My dad broke the silence. He yawned a big, long yawn. "Well, it's time to turn in. Morning'll be here before you know it." He stood up. "C'mon kids. Let's go. Time for bed." He shuffled us toward the motorhome and turned to Albert one last time. "See you in the morning." To me, it seemed as much a question as a statement.

The confidence in his voice broke into tiny little pleadings, as soon as we entered the motorhome. "Lena, why did you fight with him?" He continued in a whispery breath, "Why did you get him angry? Why?"

Sitting at the little kitchen table my mother stayed firm. "I don't care if he shoots us." She crossed her arms resolutely. "Yep, he can just shoot us in our sleep. I don't care."

I kind of do, I thought.

She continued, "He's wrong! That was a terrible fight. Muhammad Ali . . ."

"Lena . . ." My dad stood over her with a hopeless look on his face. "He just killed a man . . . killed a man!" my dad pleaded. He put his head in his hands and shook his head back and forth.

"Well, I don't care," she said, but her voice began to crack and falter. "He is wrong you know." My brother Keith and I just stared at her. My dad plopped down next to her, defeated. "Should I go apologize?" she asked.

"It's too late. I heard him go to bed." As my parents nervously whispered back and forth, they eventually decided to unwind the yarn dog I had been making around a bent wire hanger—something my grandma had shown me—and my parents used the pink string to booby-trap the motorhome. My dad agreed to sit awake with his gun, just in case Albert broke in to shoot us in our sleep. Knowing that Albert could outshoot my dad, it was difficult to drift off to sleep that night.

Clearly, Albert did not shoot us. With expected eventuality, the sun meshed light with darkness and day broke, finding us all alive. Upon exiting the motorhome, we saw Albert, who was already poking a stick at smoldering and smoking ashes. Throughout that trip, he continued to pester and prod my mother for more of a battle, but she had learned her lesson, and against all that was within her, she let him win: she gave in.

Weeks later, a surprise came to my mother in the mail. Amidst a collection of glossy, personal-looking, Elvis photos Albert had found to give her, was a final picture of Muhammad Ali with the inscription on the back: "Muhammad Ali won that fight!" With that, my mother realized that just as Albert ignited something in her, she ignited something in him too: maybe the only woman to never back down from his menacing, foreboding figure, she had gained some weird respect and friendship from him, though it wasn't the kind of friendship she exactly wanted.

We actually spent a lot of time with Albert. Most of our vacations included time with Albert in his desert home. We tried to forget about him killing a man. First of all, it was scary to contemplate, and secondly, for my family it would have been rude to hold that against him. Eventually, Albert died of a massive heart attack, while on a hunting trip in the desert. Though he tried to get his truck to the main road for help, he fell over in his cab clutching his chest with the engine running. They found him there two days later.

I think most people agree that it is imprudent to argue with a suspected killer, but what if you don't know the heart of the person you are arguing with? As I've said in the story "Chasing Elvis," "God sees not as man sees, for man looks at the outward appearance, but the Lord looks at the heart" (1 Samuel 16:7). Only God can know a man's heart, so only God can see whether or not a man has a murderous heart. I'm sure there were places that Albert chose to conduct himself uprightly and there were people who would never have suspected that he had killed someone. In fact, having been raised in the church, Albert continued to be a regular church attendee all throughout his adult life. I would assume that while he was at church, Albert was on his best behavior, never exasperating or initiating conflict with anyone.

While you might not be able to know someone else's heart, you can assuredly know your own. With this story, I want to encourage you to weed out things that incite you to unrighteous anger. I will be honest, the thing I have most in common with my mother is her quick defense of justice—defending what is right, regardless of the subject or cost. Growing up, I found this one of my mother's key attributes, so when I became old enough to have a voice, I garnered what I had learned from her and carried the torch. At school, I defended the weak; in work, I recounted the abilities of the unsung; and in life, I stood for what I devoutly believed was right. So what is the problem with this philosophy? Well, the problem with this ideology is that when human thought is the summation of right and wrong, we are left with a highly subjective sense of right and wrong.

For a while you may be able to accommodate righteousness in

your attempt to set the world straight, but after a while, self-righteous posturing becomes haughty and offensive: Let's face it, no one knows everything. There is a saying I wish I had known in my youth: "I don't even know what I don't know." The things you might vehemently defend now certainly won't hold the same veracity with maturity and age.

When I was a young college student I belonged to the National Organization of Women. I was appalled by the inequality of pay for men and women, and though that was my key sticking point, I also strongly defended a woman's right to choose abortion. By the end of my college years I had come to believe differently about abortion because I had been required to kill a midterm Japanese quail embryo as a dissection experiment in my Avian Sciences class. With the egg cracked open and the limp bird's heartbeat growing more and more faint, I knew that if I couldn't poke around at that little bird embryo, I certainly could not kill or justify the killing of a human being. In fact, quite to the professor's dismay, I began to weep for the little bird. I thrust my fist into the air in a show of bizarre solidarity for the dying bird, and was then quietly ushered out of the lab. If someone had told me how my heart would be swayed away from my staunch views, I wouldn't have believed it, but God has a way of changing us when we least expect it.

When my mother committed suicide, and as Rick and I were embroiled in a lengthy lawsuit, my trip down Anger Lane was only to be expected. I will admit I had angry, vengeful visions of our legal opponent—most of which included a mountain lion. I wished for something horrible to befall him. I hoped God would vindicate us, but I wasn't entirely opposed to doing the vindicating myself (I tell you, I am bent on giving someone the asphalt facial scrub they richly deserve!). The problem with this way of thinking is that when you meditate on angry visions, you cease giving your thoughts to God. In my opinion, you are welcoming the Evil One inside your home to sit a spell, and last I checked, no Christian wants to sit a spell with the Evil One! We are not equipped to entertain such stuff. If you think you are, please read the following verse:

Little children, make sure no one deceives you; the one who practices righteousness is righteous, just as He is righteous; the one who practices sin is of the devil; for the devil has sinned from the beginning . . . By this the children of God and the children of the devil are obvious: anyone who does not practice righteousness is not of God, nor the one who does not love his brother (1 John 3:7–10).

If you practice righteousness, you shouldn't be privy to, or accustomed to evil ways. It is simply counter-intuitive thinking, especially when you consider what it says in Romans 16:19, "I want you to be wise in what is good and innocent in what is evil." Assuming God will allow you to prevail over evil is, in many regards, testing the spirits, which we are also called to avoid doing (1 John 4:1).

God also taught us to retreat from potentially caustic people and interactions. The desire to live peacefully was the resounding lesson we learned from our interaction with someone who had no regard for God or behaving righteously. From difficult lessons learned, I deeply encourage you "If possible, so far as it depends on you, be at peace with all men. Never take your revenge, beloved, but leave room for the wrath of God, for it is written, 'Vengeance is mine, I will repay,' says the Lord" (Romans 12:17–19).

Read Proverbs 15:1–33, and answer the following questions.

Rumble in the Desert—Bible Study

1. When is the last time you engaged with someone in an unrighteous, angry way? Was your point heard or accomplished?

2. What are some practical reasons we should avoid angrily engaging with someone?

3. What are the spiritual reasons we should avoid angrily engaging with someone?

4. Read Proverbs 15:18. Considering your last argument or disagreement, were you the "hot-tempered" person or the "patient man"? How could you have handled the dispute better?

5. Why is it unacceptable for a Christ-follower to engage in malicious, vengeful thoughts of someone who has mistreated them? What would be a better way to deal with someone who is evil toward you?

Blessed Assurance
By Fanny Crosby (1873)

Blessed assurance, Jesus is mine!
O what a foretaste of glory divine!
Heir of salvation, purchase of God,
Born of His Spirit, washed in His blood.

This is my story, this is my song,
Praising my Savior, all the day long;
This is my story, this is my song,
Praising my Savior, all the day long.

Perfect submission, perfect delight,
Visions of rapture now burst on my sight;
Angels descending bring from above
Echoes of mercy, whispers of love.

This is my story, this is my song,
Praising my Savior, all the day long;
This is my story, this is my song,
Praising my Savior, all the day long.

Perfect submission, all is at rest
I in my Savior am happy and blest,
Watching and waiting, looking above,
Filled with His goodness, lost in His love.

This is my story, this is my song,
Praising my Savior, all the day long;
This is my story, this is my song,
Praising my Savior, all the day long.

Dear Reader,

This is, indeed, my story. We all have stories. Stories are told for different reasons, but I hope to glorify God and encourage others to love Christ with my stories. I believe with all my heart that God and faith in Jesus Christ can save your eternal soul. I believe that God and faith in Christ can give you eternal hope, no matter what your circumstances. If he can save me, He can save and give hope to anyone. The hope you find in Christ will never wane, it will not grow old or faint; it is eternal hope that never falters, ever.

If you've ever been hurt by someone who claimed the name of Jesus, ignore the hurtful person, and seek the comfort of Christ, "for God did not send his Son into the world to condemn the world, but to save the world through him" (John 3:17).

What do you need to do to be saved by faith? "If you declare with your mouth, 'Jesus is Lord,' and believe in your heart that God raised him from the dead, you will be saved" (Romans 10:9).

Think on this: Most people spend weeks planning their yearly vacations and days dreaming about it before and after, yet eternity is much longer than a yearly vacation. How much time do you spend thinking about eternity? You will end up somewhere. Be sure it's where you want to go. If you can give a yearly vacation your time, money, thoughts, and planning, I encourage you to give your plans for eternity much more than that.

"Lead me by your truth and teach me, for you are the God who saves me. All day long I put my hope in you" (Psalm 25:5).

Much Love,
Michelle